Promising Practices
for Teachers to Engage Families
of English Language Learners

A volume in
Family–School–Community Partnership Series
Diana B. Hiatt-Michael, *Series Editor*

Family–School–Community Partnership Series

Diana B. Hiatt-Michael
Series Editor

Promising Practices for Teachers to Engage Families of English Language Learners
Edited by Diana Hiatt-Michael

Promising Practices Connecting Schools to Families of Children with Special Needs
Edited by Diana Hiatt-Michael

Promising Practices for Family Involvement in Schooling Across the Continents
Edited by Diana Hiatt-Michael

Promising Practices for Family Involvement in Schools
Edited by Diana Hiatt-Michael

Promising Practices to Connect Schools with the Community
Edited by Diana Hiatt-Michael

Promising Practices
for Teachers to Engage Families
of English Language Learners

Edited by

Diana B. Hiatt-Michael
Pepperdine University

INFORMATION AGE PUBLISHING, INC.
Charlotte, NC • www.infoagepub.com

Library of Congress Cataloging-in-Publication Data

Promising practices for teachers to engage families of English language
learners / edited by Diana B. Hiatt-Michael.
    p. cm. – (Family school community partnership issues)
 Includes bibliographical references.
 ISBN-13: 978-1-59311-660-6 (pbk.)
 ISBN-13: 978-1-59311-661-3 (hardcover)
 1. Education–Parent participation–United States. 2. Home and
school–United States. 3. Parent-teacher relationships–United States. 4.
Limited English proficient students–Education–United States. 5. English
language–Study and teaching–Foreign speakers. I. Hiatt-Michael, Diana B.
 LB1048.5.P768 2007
 429'.0071–dc22

                                                    2007023800

Printed in the United States of America

*This monograph is dedicated to my husband John W. Michael,
whose encouragement, devotion, and support are invaluable.*

CONTENTS

ACKNOWLEDGMENTS

Welcome to the fifth monograph in the Family–School–Community Series. This volume was specifically designed for beginning teachers who are working with families of English language learners (ELL). We created this monograph to meet numerous requests for research-supported promising practices for teachers who work with ELL and their families. Throughout the chapters, we present a plethora of ideas supported by research that are relevant to all educators and community members.

The authors of this monograph worked as a team under my facilitation to coordinate chapters and inter-connect ideas. Each chapter was the responsibility of the author(s), but all chapters were intensively critiqued by authors of the other chapters. Each author generously shared wisdom and insights. The resultant volume has been the work and responsibility of this team.

Collectively, we wish to extend our deepest appreciation to the various teachers, principals, researchers, and other educators who shared their work with us. This volume would not have been possible without their many contributions to promising practices and research support. In addition, we wish to express our appreciation to Mary Cornish, for her outside review and thoughtful notes across the chapters. We extend special recognition to my research assistant Carol Ann Pyburn who served as assistant editor throughout the process. She carefully attended to the many details required of an edited book. We treasure her enthusiasm and dedication to our work.

Chris Ferguson adds a thundering expression of gratitude to the many ELL parents who offered their wisdom and commitment to the education of ELL students.

Hsui-Zu Ho acknowledges her husband William A. Below for his patience and continuing support of her work. Other authors extend their appreciation to their spouses/families for their understanding throughout the writing process.

CHAPTER 1

ENGAGING ENGLISH LANGUAGE LEARNER FAMILIES AS PARTNERS

Diana Hiatt-Michael

This monograph is a guide for teachers working with English language learners (ELL) and their parents. The underlying premise of this monograph is that you as a teacher are central to the academic success of the children in your classroom. Research has continued to remind policymakers that the quality of school life is dependent on the professional capability of the persons who are teachers in the classroom (Falk, 2006).

Much of the success of your efforts relies on your ability to tap into the rich resources of your students' families. Numerous studies point out that your students will achieve increased satisfaction in school and higher academic achievement when you include the parents in curricular planning, implementation, and evaluation (Harvard Family Research Project, 2006/2007; Henderson & Mapp, 2002; Jeynes, 2007).

Promising Practices for Teachers to Engage Families of English Language Learners, pages 1–10
Copyright © 2007 by Information Age Publishing
All rights of reproduction in any form reserved.

FUNDS OF KNOWLEDGE

What Teachers Bring to the School-Home Relationship

Moll's concept—"funds of knowledge"—provides a means to connect what the teacher of ELL students and ELL families bring to the teacher-family partnership (Moll & Gonzalez, 1997). Every year teachers are assigned new classes of students. In these classes, each child arrives to the teacher as a unique individual, comprising genetic imprinting and environmental revisions. Child development provides a large body of research for teachers. Such knowledge provides a template of general expectations for students. Teachers interpret the behavior of new students in light of previously acquired knowledge of child development. In addition, teachers have stored up experiences about children through their work with prior students. The teacher can retrieve behavior that worked in a prior situation to apply with a child who seems to have a similar need. Lastly, teachers have spent significant time and training in teacher education, reading educational materials, and participating in staff development opportunities. They bring this fund of knowledge and life experiences in education to the teaching situation with a child. However, their knowledge is also grounded in their culture and the language that express that culture.

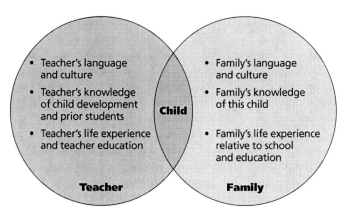

The teacher possesses a reservoir of information and skills that grows with every new encounter. But, each student is unique and has a spent significant portion of their life within the family and the family's culture. A large reservoir of information regarding each child remains within the child's family members.

What Families Bring to the Home-School Relationship

Families serve as a fund of knowledge regarding the individual child. Family members possess intimate details about your student, such as the child's experiences, medical concerns, and interests. As families, parents and children have known fears, been worried, experienced joys, and shared laughter. Parents perceive what motivates the child, what keeps the child from participating in school, and how to bring out the best qualities of each child.

In addition, families also possess a fund of knowledge regarding their culture and their language that is grounded in that culture. In order to develop an understanding of families and the community, Hamilton Boone (2007) reminds teachers of ELL that they should remain attentive to the cultural support needs of those outside the teacher's own cultural sphere. She recommends that teachers continually stay tuned in to how communication attempts may or may not register with persons who do not share their cultural background. While all cultures are not completely different, as teachers, it is necessary to explore how perceived similarities differ as culture and language are inextricably intertwined (Klopf, 1995), and every culture has needs that activate and /or motivate our communicative behaviors (Barna, 1994).

A school administrator (Colombo, 2006) described the academic benefits of Parent Partnership for Achieving Literacy (PAL). PAL was designed to create increased awareness by teachers to the needs of ELL families. Teachers participated in professional development activities along with ELL parents. PAL has been operating for more than four years at the K–3 level with regular, high attendance. Responding to a standardized survey, the teachers indicated that students whose parents were in the PAL program made progress in reading, verbal communication, and classroom behavior.

In addition, families can provide resources for their own child and other students in your classroom. Such resources include donations of time and talent. Parents are a low-cost means to improve academic achievement. For example, parents can assist in language interpretation, locate appropriate culture and language materials, organize a cultural event, or secure donations from community businesses and agencies. Utilizing parent knowledge and resources provides a free benefit to schools (refer to Chapters 4, 5, 6, and 7 for numerous examples).

Teacher as Initiator of Two-Way Dialogue

Successful and satisfying relationships between teachers and their students' families depend upon a two-way dialogue. Hamilton Boone (2007) asserts that:

> When communication between teachers and parents is clear, students have a far better chance of succeeding in their academic environment. The constant challenge for the teacher of English learners is to establish and nurture a symbiotic relationship between the classroom and students' homes. (p. 1)

A review of parent involvement across continents revealed that all parents value quality education for their children (Hiatt-Michael, 2005). Parents from every culture want the best education that is possible for their children. Parents look to teachers for answers regarding their child's social adjustment and success in learning. However, when language barriers separate the teachers and the parents, parents may be hesitant to begin communication and visit the classroom teacher according to one ELL Coordinator in Los Angeles (R. Jaber-Ansari, personal communication, March 19, 2007). In addition, these parents may consider the school's expectations of their role to be similar to the school-home relationship in their culture; they may not believe that parents are welcome or even should be active at the school site. Therefore, teachers must initiate the contact and reach out to the parents (Hoover-Dempsey & Walker, 2002; Hiatt & Johnstone, 1997).

The importance of your reaching out to the families of your students cannot be stated strongly enough. As the child's teacher, you are the linchpin to positive home-school support of students' academic achievement (Mawhinney & Sagan, 2007). Your efforts have to overcome the perceived barriers by parents. Sosa (1997) reports that these include uncertainty about the parents' roles with the school, anxiety about what teachers think about them as parents, concerns related to educational policies, unhappiness about their communication limitations, and dissatisfaction with their home environment.

Since both teachers and family members possess funds of knowledge that should be shared for the benefit of the student, during any teacher–parent dialogue, bidirectional learning will occur for teachers and the parents as they share their knowledge of the student. Chapter 2 describes the underlying research on home-school relationships featuring work related to ELL and the importance of building home-school relationships based upon caring and respect for these two funds of knowledge. Some recommendations are to regularly invite parent opinion, solicit their input and feedback, ask parents how they are doing, and request whether or not their child is getting what he/she needs from school.

Teachers should assume the responsibility to initiate this dialogue before formal instruction begins. At this time, you should consider ways to connect and establish positive relationships with your students' families. Techniques to reach ELL families include sending flyers, newsletters, positive notes, and telephone calls in the spoken language of family members.

Also, spend time to understand life in the surrounding community (refer to Chapter 3), meet families in the child's homes (see Chapter 4, home visits), and open your classroom as a way to reach out to families (go to Chapter 4, open house before school begins). Your task is to begin the conversation and to bridge the language barrier, which over time will develop into two-way dialogue. The goal of such dialogue is to build personal relationships between the school and the home that foster student satisfaction in school and educational achievement.

IMPORTANCE OF NONVERBAL COMMUNICATION

Nonverbal communication reflects your inner feelings. Gestures, facial expression, and body language affect communication more than words (Bennett & Bennett, 2004). Nonverbal communication is powerful in any setting, but nonverbal communication becomes critical with ELL families. Appropriate nonverbal communication can bridge the language barrier or widen the chasm between you and your ELL family members. A bow and soft smile to a new Japanese family express a courtesy to them. A concerned look, outstretched hand, and relaxed body translate as a personal interest to a Hispanic family. In Oman, a small country in the Middle East, a broad smile, open posture, direct eye contact, and no extension of hand welcomes the newcomer. To western Africans, new faces should share a meal and conversation before any business is transacted.

Many new teachers express a lack of confidence to work in a culture different from their own. Such a sense of uncertainty can generate negative emotions of fear, anxiety, and anger. These strong emotions are difficult emotions to camouflage. The more you observe, listen, and follow the cultural patterns demonstrated by your ELL family members, you will better connect with your ELL family members. The inherent concerns that may hinder communication are reduced and your ability to cross the language barrier will improve. Thus, your confidence will increase in bilingual and bicultural communication.

IMMIGRANTS AND ELL

Although not all ELL students and their parents can be classified as first generation immigrants, most ELL students are either children of first generation immigrants or new immigrants recently received by family members already residing in America. Children of immigrants comprise 20% of children in America (Suarez-Orozco & Suarez-Orozco, 2001, p. 1). These immigrants and their children primarily migrate to urban centers. These families arrive with varied backgrounds in socioeconomic level, use of English, and prior educational experiences. These differences will determine their choice of a new area to live in and their ability to navigate in the new school system. Some families have left areas of strife and trauma. They will be carrying these experiences with them to the new school.

The largest number of immigrants is Hispanic arriving from Mexico, Central America, and South America. This Hispanic population also represents the largest dropout rate in America. Although this monograph will address working with diverse groups of ELL parents, more examples will address the needs of Hispanic parents.

English language proficiency may differ between the immigrant parent and their children. In some districts with strong bilingual programs such as Lennox, California, students may be attaining a strong command of both languages, but their parents may continue to feel more comfortable in their first language. In areas of high density of any given language group, families can successfully function in their native language. Signs, messages, and instructions are written in their language. Clerks and other personnel speak their language. Thus, these parents do not have a vital need to acquire English and may prefer to communicate in their first language.

In Lennox, California, a career fair for parents and students in a new immigrant Hispanic school revealed the differences in language usage between the immigrant parents and their children (Hiatt-Michael, 2007). The LMS6 Career Fair was targeted for middle school children. Analysis of their ELL records indicated that less than 20% were limited English speakers. Thus, the presenters who shared their careers addressed the student audience in English. However, responses to career fair flyers in Spanish and English revealed that almost all of the parents preferred to communicate in Spanish. Thus, the creators developed separate sessions for the parents delivered in Spanish.

And, not all immigrants may consider themselves as ELL. Some have come from countries in which English was included as a part of the curriculum from early or late elementary school age. For example, in India, the school curriculum is in English. In Russia and Oman, primary students may acquire English. Private schools across countries often include English in their basic curriculum, beginning in preschool, primary, or elementary levels and continuing for years. Thus, teachers cannot assume that new immigrant parents may not be fluent in English.

DEFINITIONS OF TERMS

For this monograph, we will utilize terms in a particular way. The following figure depicts our definition of these terms.

Culture is the system of shared beliefs, values, customs, behaviors, and artifacts that the members of society use to cope with their world and with one another, and that are transmitted from generation to generation through learning (B and P, p. 7).

English language learners (ELL) are children and adults for whom English is a second language and a language in which they are still acquiring vocabulary, grammar, and inflection.

Family is an intimate social group based on kinship with responsibility for rearing children who are students in public schools in America.

Home-school relationships are the formal and informal connections between the family and the school.

Immigrant parents are adults who are foreign-born and who have permanently immigrated to the United States.

Immigrant students are children and youth born to immigrant parents prior to coming to the United States.

Parent refers to the biological parent and/or the designated custodian of the student.

ORGANIZATION OF THIS MONOGRAPH

This promising practices monograph provides research support and a plethora of ways to connect and utilize parents of ELL. This monograph utilizes a collection of major research studies and applies their findings to classroom practice. Ferguson's discussion in Chapter 2 provides the background theory from The National Center for Family and Community Connections with Schools created in 2000 by Southwest Educational Development Laboratory (SEDL). SEDL is one of 10 Regional Education Laboratories in United States funded by U.S. the Department of Education. Their publications *A New Wave of Evidence* in 2002 and *Diversity: School Family and Community Connections* in 2003 summarize the significant research up to their dates of publication (Boethel, 2003; Henderson & Mapp, 2002). As indicated in their review of research, parents of ELL experienced more barriers because of the limited or lack of use of the English language. Chapter 2 provides an overview of the research studies showing the importance of parent involvement for student academic success and satisfaction in school. Your grasp of this information will guide you to feel and behave in ways that promote caring and respect for ELL family members.

Garcia-Ramos in Chapter 3 provides ways to collect information regarding the surrounding community. Your teaching position will probably bring you to a culture that is different from the one in which you live. Your work interfaces with the culture of the community through the students and their parents. She suggests a way to analyze the community as well as a means to help ELL parents know the school facility and services.

Hiatt-Michael and Purrington in Chapter 4 guide you in ways to reach out to parents. To assist you in getting acquainted with each family of a student in your classroom, these authors recommend creating a Classroom Open House before school officially commences and plan home visits before or during the early part of the school year. This chapter also addresses your collaboration with school parent liaisons, parent councils, and preparing a Parent Communication Action Plan.

In Chapter 5, Ho, Fox, and Gonzales detail a wide array of specific practices and ideas to help ELL families feel comfortable in your classroom. This array encompasses preparing signs and materials in the families' native language, specific ways to communicate with parents from diverse cultures, parent job lists, and encouraging parents to actively participate in the classroom. They lay out a series of suggestions for successful teacher-ELL parent conferences. Lastly, they reveal best practices for the required Parent Open House.

Gonzales, Ho, and Fox continue in Chapter 6 to explain types of parent programs. These programs include how to navigate the school system, improving adult literacy, developing computer literacy, and developing parenting skills. The authors describe how to create a parent resource center. They recommend ways to promote parent-to-parent relationships through grade level events, parent clubs, and community study groups. A primary concern shared by parents and teachers is homework; the authors support options with significant research on this topic.

In the final chapter, Munter, Tinajero, and del Campo illustrate ways for parents to assume roles of leadership in your classroom and the school. Their practices include ways to impact the school curriculum, lead in community outreach, provide service learning opportunities, assist in a classroom academic event such as The Family Story Power Writing Workshop, and participating on the bilingual advisory committee. Their chapter concludes with recommendations for professional development opportunities for parents as school leaders.

Each chapter reveals a panoply of suggested classroom practices to reach out and involve parents in your classroom and school life. Our intent is that our suggested practices, supported by research, will provide a strong foundation for your knowledge of parent involvement as related to working with parents who are ELL. We hope that our array of promising practices will generate new ideas for you and your particular situation.

REFERENCES

Barna, L. M. (1994). Stumbling blocks in intercultural communication. In L. A. Samovar & R. Porter (Eds.), *Intercultural communication: A reader* (7th ed., pp. 337–46). Belmont: CA: Wadsworth.

Bates, D. G., & Plog, F. (1990). *Cultural anthropology.* New York: McGraw-Hill.

Bennett, J. M., & Bennett, M. J. (2004). Developing intercultural sensitivity: An integrative approach to global and domestic diversity. In D. Landis, J. M. Bennett, & M. J. Bennett (Eds.), *Handbook of intercultural training* (3rd ed., pp. 147–165). Thousand Oaks, CA: Sage.

Boethel, M. (2003). *Diversity: School, family and community connections.* Austin, TX: National Center for Family & Community Connections with Schools, Southwest Educational Development Laboratory.

Colombo, M. W. (2006). Building school partnerships with culturally and linguistically diverse families. *Phi Delta Kappa, 88,* 312–318.

Falk, B. (2006). A conversation with Lee Shulman. *The New Educator, 2,* 73–82.

Hamilton Boone, J. H. (2007). *Outside the cultural comfort zone: Developing an understanding of families and community through intercultural communication.* Unpublished manuscript, Pepperdine University, Los Angeles, CA.

Harvard Family Research Project. (2006/2007, Winter). Family involvement in elementary school children's education. *Family Involvement Makes a Difference, 2.*

Henderson, A. T., & Mapp, K. L. (2002). *A new wave of evidence: The impact of school, family, and community connections on student achievement.* Austin, TX: National Center for Family & Community Connections with Schools, Southwest Educational Development Laboratory.

Hiatt-Michael, D. B., Goldman, N., & Heredia, R. (2007). *Constructing LMS6 middle school career day.* Unpublished manuscript, Pepperdine University, Los Angeles, CA.

Hiatt-Michael, D. B. (2005). Global overview of family-school involvement. In D. B. Hiatt-Michael (Ed.), *Promising practices for family involvement in schooling across the continents.* Charlotte, NC: Information Age Publishing.

Hiatt, D. B., & Johnstone, T. R. (1997). *Development of a school-based parent center for low-income new immigrants.* Symposium conducted at the American Educational Research Association Annual Meeting, Chicago, IL.

Hoover-Dempsey, K.V., & Walker, J. M.T. (2002). Family-school communication. Retrieved on December 6, 2006, at http://www.nashville.k12.us/general_info_folder/hooeverdempsey_walker.pdf

Jeynes, W. H. (2007). A meta-analysis of the relation of parental involvement to urban elementary school student academic achievement. *Urban Education 42,* 82–110.

Klopf, D. W. (1995). *Intercultural encounters: The fundamentals of intercultural communication.* Englewood, CO: Morton Publishing Company.

Mawhinney, T. S., & Sagan, L. L. (2007). The power of personal relationships. *Phi Delta Kappan, 88,* 460–464.

Moll, L., & Gonzalez, N. (1997). Teachers as social scientists: Learning about culture from household research. In P. M. Hall (Ed.), *Race, ethnicity and multiculturalism* (pp. 89–114). New York: Garland.

Sosa, A. S. (1997/Spring & Summer) Involving Hispanic parents in educational activities through collaborative relationships. *Bilingual Research Journal, 2,* 103-111.

Suarez-Orozco, C., & Suarez-Orozco, M. M. (2001). *Children of immigration.* Cambridge, MA: Harvard University Press.

CHAPTER 2

BUILDING MEANINGFUL RELATIONSHIPS

Caring and Respect

Chris Ferguson

> ...As a learner, a teacher, and a teacher-educator, I have experienced the powers of good and bad teaching, the manifold challenges of doing it well, and the awesome complexities of understanding all of the contextual factors which influence why and how we teach. Such a complex art cannot be described in simple terms, and the problems we face do not admit simple solutions. (Mayher, 1990, p. 1)

In this quote, Mayher describes both the compelling and frustrating nature of teaching. While it can be wonderfully rewarding, teaching can also be a mind-boggling process. No matter how well trained the teacher, there are no easy answers to insure that every child is successful. However, within this quote lies a kernel of wisdom for teachers as they create their classroom learning culture: the need to understand the contextual factors that influence a child's educational experience.

On the first day of school, teachers begin with a sense of anticipation but also apprehension. We are eager to meet our new students, knowing that each child will be unlike previous students. To help every child reach full potential, we need to know how to reach that child—*What makes that*

Promising Practices for Teachers to Engage Families of English Language Learners, pages 11–31
Copyright © 2007 by Information Age Publishing

child tick? Sometimes, we know exactly how to connect with a child. Sometimes, we falter. Fortunately, in our work, we are not alone. Every teacher expects to get help from colleagues, but there is another source of support that we often neglect to tap into—the students' families. Family members can provide information about the child's home and community context and reinforcement for classroom instruction that can make the difference between a child being successful in school or not. For this reason, a primary task for teachers, at the beginning of each and every school year, is building a bridge between students' families and the classroom. Everyone benefits when teachers involve families in supporting their children's education (Table 2.1). Therefore, this monograph will explore important issues related to this topic and include strategies that build strong home-school connections with careful attention to strategies teachers can employ to cross the language barrier.

TABLE 2.1
Benefits of Involvement

When teachers and families are able to collaboratively implement effective school, family, community programs commonly there are benefits to all school stakeholders:

Students	additional support for learning
Family Members	new knowledge and skills in supporting their children's education and their own education as well as a better understanding of the school system and its goals and needs
Schools	support for school goals, including increased support for student achievement, positive teacher-student interactions, and additional resources
Teachers	greater understanding of the perspectives of family and community members
Community	support for outreach efforts by working with community organizations facilitate family member access to these efforts

Boethel, 2003; Henderson & Mapp, 2002

MEANINGFUL INVOLVEMENT

Though language is certainly not the only contextual factor that can impact a student's success in school, it is a significant issue. In America as well as in other countries, teachers commonly need to address the needs of immigrant students who are new to the culture and to English as the dominant language (Suarez-Orozco & Suarez-Orozco, 2001). The families of these children are just as eager to have their children succeed in school as

English-speaking parents, but also commonly misunderstand what is said to them as the following quote demonstrates:

> I couldn't understand what the teacher was trying to communicate when she commented on my daughter's performance. I particularly recall two confusing comments that this teacher made: "Your daughter is very sociable," and "Your daughter is outstanding in..." My tendency as a Mexican mother was to feel very happy she was sociable; after all that was what I was fostering. However, I did not know what to do about her being "outstanding"; I had tried to teach my daughter not to "show off," but it seemed that it was not working. (first grader's mother)

To be effective in addressing the needs of ELLS, we need to employ special methods to bridge the language barrier between home and school. Scribner, Young, and Pendroza (1999) provide five strategies to frame our work to foster positive home-school relationships:

- *Build on cultural values*—Different cultures have different expectations about the educational roles of family members, teachers, the wider community, and students. Unless we are aware of these cultural implications, we may actually contribute to a child's lack of success, instead of contributing to achievement.
- *Make personal contact with families*—Too often, teachers and family members neglect personal contact. Time, language, work schedules, geography, or other barriers get in the way of contact. However, the power that can come from successful one-on-one meetings can make significant difference.
- *Foster communication with families*—Again, time, language, work schedules, geography, or other barriers get in the way of communication. However, families cannot be helpful if they don't have the right information.
- *Create a warm environment for families*—Just as honey draws more flies in the parable, providing a comfortable environment for families encourages them to engage in their children's education. Those school-family involvement programs that create a welcoming environment will draw in a wealth of resources for the school.
- *Facilitate structural accommodation for families*—Language, culture, beliefs, religion, experience, education, and a host of other factors can create barriers to participation. For families to be involved, the activities and access to information have to be designed to allow them to participate. This can only happen when both teachers and families have engaged in activities that allow the free exchange of information and beliefs.

When schools open their doors to family members and teachers actively and personally reach out to the families of their students, a new culture emerges. This culture fosters new patterns of interactions between teachers and families and supports families as they engage in their children's education (Johnstone & Hiatt, 1997; López, 2001; Rimm-Kaufman, Pianta, Cox, & Bradley, 2003). As teacher-family interactions increase in frequency, teachers begin to feel more comfortable in contacting family members, and families are more likely to contact teachers with questions. These opportunities naturally promote understanding of each other's needs and result in caring and respectful relationships among all involved (Ferguson, 2005a, 2006; Henderson & Mapp, 2002). These relationships are a key element of effective family involvement programs (Alder, 2004; Birch & Ferrin, 2002; Boethel, 2002, 2003; Ferguson, 2005b; Hoover-Dempsey & Sandler, 2005). Exploring the perspectives of all those involved by sharing information about educational experiences and backgrounds is the first step in building relationships (Paratore, 2006; Paratore, Melzi, & Krol-Sinclair, 1999).

THROUGH THE EYES OF THE TEACHER

If the research demonstrates that teacher-family connections have value, why are not teachers actively engaging in these efforts? While there is no one single cause, there is clear evidence that teachers often resist involvement because they assume that the efforts will not result in additional support for student learning or that parents do not want to be involved in a meaningful way. They often feel the families of their students lack care and respect for the teacher's role in promoting learning. In reality, it is not a lack of caring and respect; it is more likely to be a lack of communication.

Though numerous studies have found that family members do care about their children's success in school and want to support them in their school work (Collignon, Men, & Tan, 2001; Fan, 2001; Goldenberg, Gallimore, Reese, & Garnier, 2001), teachers often state that their efforts to involve students' families do not produce desired results. In fact, Smrekar and Cohen-Vogel (2001) found that teachers commonly feel that students' family members are apathetic or unsupportive because they do not actively engage in programs or efforts that teachers plan and implement. In these cases, the teachers feel that parents are not supporting their children's education or satisfying the role that teachers have defined for family members.

For example, a teacher might ask that a family member read with the student each night. However, what happens if contextual factors in the home prevent the parent from meeting the request? There might be no one in the home has the needed facility with English, or the family members who do have the skills are working a night shift. There may not be anyone in the home who can adequately complete this task. When the child comes to school the next day without doing the assignment, the teacher might assume the adults in the home do not care about their child's education—while in reality, the student and family were unable to fulfill the request.

Commonly, teachers list the following types of efforts as appropriate for families: helping with homework in reading or math, attending meetings, or supporting discipline and attendance policies. These requests typically take the form of a one-way communication by letter or phone call from teacher to family member. It is also common for teachers to fail to make accommodations for language or cultural diversity when assigning tasks. The wide array of possible contextual factors in our students' lives can create barriers to active family engagement in supporting learning through tasks such as these or others.

When teachers have limited contextual knowledge about students, their assumptions can lead to discord and avoidance, rather than improved communication (Birch & Ferrin, 2002; Rodríguez-Brown, Li, & Albom, 1999). Over time, these failed communication attempts create an ever-widening rift and may lead to an even more divisive atmosphere where effective school-family involvement becomes impossible. In these situations, teachers often react by assigning blame for problems on the family of the child or assign limited home activities because of perceived families' lack of ability or interest. Once these blaming and conciliatory behaviors are established as normal, miscommunication and a lack of coordinated actions become pervasive. Teachers feel more and more frustrated with the lack of family member response, while family members feel more and more convinced that schools do not care about them or their children. The negative atmosphere prevents "authentic, meaningful, and growth-promoting communication" to foster an atmosphere of trust building that is necessary to stop the miscommunication (Swick, 2003, p. 275).

Moreover, when teachers use one-way communication exclusively, they fail to recognize the powerful supports for learning that come from within the *household's funds of knowledge*: the way common home activities can support learning (Moll & Greenberg, 1990, p. 323). The Funds of Knowledge approach builds on the "lived experiences" of children (Gonzáles & Moll, 2002, p. 623). In this approach, teachers institutionalize home learning as part of the classroom lesson, and they help students and families to realize that their daily actions can become a part of a child's learning. Unfortunately, teachers tend to value traditional or school-based learning rather than learning that takes place outside of the classroom or the school—the "extended zone of proximal development" (Moll & Greenberg, 1990, p.

323). For example, a teacher can use statement problems about local demographic changes to introduce ratio or a teacher can involve local craftsmen (including family members) to partner with students to demonstrate how ratio is used in home building, baking, or canning.

Obviously, both methods offer students an opportunity to apply their knowledge to real world situations. However, the second method not only builds on *funds of knowledge*, it also fosters shared partnerships among all who have a stake in a child's education; information and actions flow to *and* from the teacher. As is typical of an approach taking advantage of *funds of knowledge*, the content knowledge that children need is found in the common activities around them as well as in the school building. These types of learning experiences offer multiple benefits:

1. Students gain support for their learning.
2. Teachers are able to tap into new forms of instructional support.
3. Family members learn to use their own knowledge and skill to support their children's learning.
4. The learning culture and environment expand to include everyday activities.

This type of effort is only possible when teachers are able to embrace multiple perspectives. When teachers know both the perspectives of the family members as well as their own perspective, they have increased their power of understanding (Ferguson, 2005b). Such knowledge allows teacher and family members to take on joint responsibility for student learning. These efforts foster caring and respect among all involved.

As we see in the following experience of Ms. Haslet, all participants' reactions and situational understanding are affected by the fund of knowledge that they bring to the situation. Lack of contextual understanding of others' point of view can lead to miscommunication.

Before the parent conference, Ms. Haslet checked her records prepared for the conference. In one stack, she had copies of every newsletter she had sent home with her students. In another, she had copies of invitations to the family math nights. Beside the stacks, she had typed notes about every request sent home, letter mailed, and phone call made. She was determined that she was going to make these parents realize that the school expected parents to support their children's education.

There was a knock on the door; Ms. Haslet put a smile on her face and invited her student Marija to bring her family into the classroom. She noted that both parents had come as well as a young man, whom she quickly learned was a cousin. After quick introductions, Ms. Haslet asked everyone to sit down and began her carefully prepared speech. She used the newsletters and invitations to reinforce her statements about the need and expectation for parents to be involved in their children's education. Then, she began to tell them the additional things she wanted the parents to do: read with Marija, check her spelling, take her to the library, and so on. Toward the end of her presentation, she looked up and saw a growing befuddlement on the adults' faces.

She paused. The cousin began to immediately speak to the parents in Serb-Croatian. Though she knew this family was from the Balkans, she had assumed that the parents spoke English since English was commonly spoken in Europe. Finally, the cousin turned to her and said, "I've told them what you said, but I don't think you understand their home situation. I speak English because my family moved to the United States when I was ten. Marija and her parents have only been here for 3 years. They came with our grandparents. Marija's parents are supporting six family members. Marija's father is working two jobs and her mother works night shifts. Each time you send a note or leave a message, they ask me to explain it to them. They understand what you are asking but feel that some of your requests are impossible for now. When you ask that a parent read with Marija, I do it. However, your note asks for the parent who reads with her to sign in the blank. They do not wish to lie, so there is no name in the blank even though an adult is reading with her. I came today to help you understand their situation. Let me tell you how they are helping Marija . . ."

Ms. Haslet sat back and listened. These were not uncaring adults who needed to be taught responsibility; they were loving parents who wanted their child to succeed. Soon, she began to jot down ideas, names of contacts, and questions to ask. She had just learned what research has shown: families are interested in their children's academic success regardless of ethnicity, culture, or economic status, although they may not know how to help their children or may feel incapable of assisting them the way teachers asks.

While this story demonstrates the complexity of initiating family involvement with diverse populations, it also reveals the power of one-on-one dialogue. By engaging in a face-to-face meeting, the teachers and the family members were able to explore the assumptions and experiences that each person brings into a meeting and surface contextual factors that can lead to misunderstandings. Because immigrant families are often communicating in a new language and are unfamiliar with the school system, direct interactions are an essential strategy to insure that all those involved understand the expectations for parents and students (Adler, 2004; Suarez-Orozco & Suarez-Orozco, 2001). However, adopting a more inclusive process is not without its difficulties. Teachers' beliefs drive their actions (Elbaz, 1991; Elliot & Drake, 1999; Ferguson, 2004; Hamachek, 1999). If they believe family involvement will have value for their students, they will foster school-family connections. If they do not, they will avoid the practice and rely solely on school-based programs.

Before we can create a culture that fosters family involvement and accept the views of others, we need to explore our own cultural values and our role in promoting learning (Greenfield, Quiroz, & Raeff, 2000). We can do this as individuals or with other educators, but if we involve families in this process, we will accomplish two goals at the same time: clarifying our own culture values and educational responsibilities and taking a first step in building an effective involvement program. By asking families to join in this process, we have the opportunity to explore our own educational values and roles as the families also explore theirs. As a result, we gain greater understanding of each other's cultural values and the roles we accept in promoting learning. These understandings become the foundation for strong teacher-family relationships. These relationships will foster caring and respect among all involved and become the catalyst for the changes we need to make in classrooms, schools, and homes if we are to provide the support our students need.

For teachers, Meyer (1999) describes this shift in beliefs as *transformative teaching and learning*. Over time as teachers explore new ideas and their own beliefs, they create or discover strategies that align to their changing beliefs. However, Meyer also says teachers will experience discomfort or disequilibrium as they adopt new ideas because they are questioning long-held beliefs. For families, the experience may also be uncomfortable at times. If we want these efforts to be successful, we need to insure that we recognize their discomfort and do what we can to provide a supportive culture for them.

THROUGH THE EYES OF THE FAMILY

Just as teachers commonly misread the actions of parents or other adults in the home, family members also misunderstand the actions of teachers. Families often limit their active engagement because they lack experience and knowledge about schools or education. They typically do not know their children's teachers well enough to feel comfortable communicating with them. Because of their limited interactions with teachers, they often assume that teachers do not value or respect their contributions to their children's education. When family members do not speak English, the possible problems are often more pronounced.

Numerous studies have explored the contextual issues that impact if and how families engage in their children's education (Birch & Ferrin, 2002; Dearing, McCartney, Weiss, Kreider, & Simpkins, 2004; Fan, 2001; Fantuzzo, McWayne, & Perry, 2004; Leibhaman, Alexander, Johnson, Neitzel, & Reis-Menrie, 2005; Levine & Trickett, 2000; Todd & Higgins, 1998). However, anticipating families' perspectives can be complicated. For example, a math assignment that asks students to survey the adults in the neighborhood and report the median and mean age of those surveyed may be threatening in a neighborhood comprising recent immigrants who are actually refugees from a repressive government. Our lives are often so different from the lives of our students and their families that we cannot foresee all of these types of situations. We can, however, open our minds to possible factors. In their study of immigrant families, Suárez-Orozco and Suárez-Orozco' (2001) provide a list of factors that limit families' active engagement to support student learning:

1. In the home countries of some adults, there is often a strict barrier between school and home, and parents are not encouraged to cross over this line. Whereas in the United States, teachers expect that families will be an active part of their children's educational success.

2. Family members who are poorly educated often feel ill equipped to support or advocate for their child's academic success.

3. It is also not unusual for recent immigrants to the United States to work multiple jobs; this essentially prohibits their involvement in any school activities or in at home support activities.

4. Family members who do not speak English sufficiently or who perceive their English skills are too limited to engage in conversation also find navigating the school system difficult.

Though these identified factors may apply to many families, there are a multitude of other factors that encourage or discourage families to engage in their children's educations. Differences in the family structure, culture, ethnic background, social class, age and gender can also affect the nature of family involvement. A family member's lack of understanding about the policies, or practices, and expectations of schools can be a significant barrier to fully engaging in school-family efforts (Chrispeels & Rivero, 2001; Collignon et al., 2001; Péna, 2000). Attempting to explain these influences, McLoyd, Hill, and Dodge (2005) describe the array of factors impacting family involvement as a series of unseen forces that cascade through school-family events. Each factor is distinctive, yet there is an overarching connection among all the factors. Negotiating the intricacies of these elements is a difficult process, particularly if the teacher is not familiar with the contextual influences in the school community.

When parents are not English speakers, another nuance is added to the complexity of these efforts. As teachers plan to implement parental involvement with these parents, they need to anticipate when a translation process will have a positive or negative impact. There is not question that translation empowers parents to access the information they need. Without translation, the involvement of non-English speaking parents can be severely limited, while there is no one best method of translating, there are parent preferences and need that should be considered to insure that the translation process provided the greatest benefit. For example, if children are used as translators, are the parents being embarrasses? Though in some circumstances, the use of children as translators is natural and effective, there are occasions when parents feel uncomfortable or even humiliated. As teachers, we need to reach out to the parents and cultural group in our communities and determine the best way to translate. Do the parents prefer simultaneous translations during an event? Or would they prefer the conversation to stop periodically and hear a translation of what has been said? Do they prefer to sit as a group and hear the translation as a group or interspersed throughout the room? (Hall & Sham, 1998; Vasquez, Pease-Alvarez, & Shannon, 1994).

Just as teacher beliefs determine their choices to reach to family members, a family member's underlying beliefs impact the actions they take to support their children's education (Birch & Ferrin, 2002; Chrispeels & Rivero, 2001; Péna, 2000; Reese & Gallimore, 2000). Although research studies reflect that *families care about their children's education*, research findings suggest that *parents often do not know how to support their children's education.* When teachers reach out to families and actively engage them in activities that lead to greater understanding and shared information, they "promote" collective support of students' learning and progress (Sanders, 2000, p. 54). These types of efforts prevent the misunderstandings generated by such situations as the ones described in Ms. Haslet's vignette and provide an opportunity for those involved to develop caring and respectful relationships.

TAKING STEPS TO DEVELOP SHARED PERSPECTIVES

When families are given the right information in an appropriate way (Musti- Rao & Cartledge, 2004), they can become a valuable resource in meeting student needs (Desimone, Finn-Stevenson, & Henrich, 2000; Levine & Trickett, 2000). As the two sections of this chapter, "Through the Eyes of the Teachers" and "Through the Eyes of the Family," have demonstrated, communicating about each other's perspectives and building shared understanding is a key to effective teacher-family connections. While there is no single method of accomplishing this goal, there are strategies and lessons that can be helpful. For example, Cooper and Christie (2005) note that district staff might see their family involvement goals as helping family members to become engaged citizens and promote effective education change. However, family members are often more likely to value goals that are tightly linked to important social and cultural issues.

In choosing communication methods consider the following questions:

Does the communication method allow for cultural differences in experience and knowledge related to working with schools and teachers?

For example, a note asking family members to participate in a mini-workshop to develop home-based literacy projects may be inappropriate if the adults at home come from a culture in which co-planning with a teacher is not accepted. Moreover, if the home language is not English, the adult might be even more apprehensive. However, if the teacher begins this process with a simple nonthreatening activity to help establish rapport with the parents, this strategy may be viable later. For example, a teacher invites families to a demonstration showcasing children's skills and knowledge with the intention of raising awareness of what types of instructional strategies are raised in the classroom and the results of that use. Based on this rapport and better understanding of the teacher's strategies, a family member may be more comfortable in supporting these instructional strategies and in working collaboratively with the teacher to address student needs at a later date.

How do teachers know their communication strategies are working?

Too often teachers assume that, if they send a note or call a child's home, they are communicating with families. Unfortunately, sending a note home with a child or via mail does not mean the note was read or that it was understood. Similarly, a nodding head or a "yes" verbal response is not always an indication of successful communication. For example, in response to a request for assistance with the weekly at home math assignments, the teacher included a sheet with a full explanation for the weekly math topic. After two months of doing this, the teacher observed very little change in the work that was done at home. She stopped sending the newsletter altogether since she felt her students' families were not interested in supporting classroom instruction. There are a multitude of reasons she might not be seeing the response she anticipated. The most obvious might be linguistic diversity, but lack of math skill or comfort with math as well as parent work schedules might be others.

While sending home an explanation might assist some family members, it is certainly not appropriate for all families. The family members, English proficient or not, may not feel they are able to read the directions sufficiently well to use them. Instead, teachers need to use several strategies to help them determine what method of communication is most useful. The teacher could have held periodic meetings in the community (not at the school) to share plans, ascertain home needs, and verify effectiveness of strategy or recruited mentors for family members among community groups or other families to help provide assistance to families who need language assistance or lack educational experience. Often, the teacher will need to use more than one strategy at a time as it is likely that one strategy will not work for all families.

Is the communicated information clear, consistent, and positive?

In the rush to meet multiple deadlines, it is not unusual for teachers to forget these three simple caveats. For example, teachers commonly use rubrics to grade assignments. If students and family members have access to the grading rubric as the work is done, students and their family members will have a better understanding of the expectations for the assignment. However, when a teacher changes the rubric format with each assignment or uses complicated grading procedures even if accompanied by detailed explanations, the family members may find these help tools confusing instead of helpful. While it is true that different kinds of assignments require different rubrics, families will make better use of them if there is consistency, so they can "master" their part of the work.

Though each of these strategies has great value, we need to remember that communication or interaction between families and teachers will "develop in dynamic nonlinear ways," and these variances cannot be anticipated (Sanders, 2000, p. 65). Sanders offers practical advice to teachers who want to foster effective teacher-family connections. Sanders suggests that the teacher: (1) allow the process to take the time needed, that is instead of rushing to accomplish goals let the process roll itself out rather than force things to happen, (2) avoid making assumptions about student families or their actions or your own practice and needs, and (3) foster sensitivity to the needs of all involved.

TYPES OF INVOLVEMENT

Numerous researchers have studied the types of family involvement that can support student learning. Epstein (2001) has defined six types of involvement that schools in the National Partnership Network commonly use across the United States. Based on their four syntheses of family and community involvement with school literature (Boethel, 2003, 2004; Henderson & Mapp, 2002; Jordan, Orozco, Averett, & Buttram, 2001), the National Center for Family and Community Connections with Schools has expanded Epstein's types of involvement to eight. The Center's eight types of involvement provide a broader explanation of how families can be engaged in schools and describe involvement that can be initiated by both the school and family members (Table 2.2). This multidirectional approach to involvement promotes shared responsibility for the education of the child among home, school, and community.

To date, research does not suggest whether the use of any one type of involvement or a combination of types will provide the greatest benefit. However, research findings indicate that efforts focused on clearly stated outcomes—ones related to student needs, are more likely to achieve posi-

TABLE 2.2
Eight Types of Family Involvement with Schools

From the School Perspective	From the Family Perspective
Fostering Supportive Home Environments	
Assisting families with parenting skills and helping to create home conditions to support student academic achievement	Seeking out and participating in activities to increase parenting skills and creating home conditions that will support academic achievement
Promoting Shared Decision Making	
Including family members as partners in school decisions	Learning about and seeking to be involved in decision-making groups
Expanding Family–School Communication	
Promoting effective two-way communications between school staff and individuals or groups of family members	Taking advantage of and fostering new avenues for communication with the school staff, local support groups, and other family members
Coordinating Resources and Services	
Uniting efforts and programs to provide services for families	Participating and learning about services, programs, and activities that can improve the family's lifestyle
Fostering Volunteer Support	
Organizing and supporting family members in their efforts to support the school and its students	Learning about and participating in programs that support the school and its students
Supporting Youth Development	
Providing services for students, such as health and physical development, creative expression, and leadership development	Seeking out and insuring that all family members—adult and child—take advantage of opportunities to address health and physical issues, learn about areas of interest, and develop leadership skills
Supporting Learning Outside of School	
Involving families and partner organizations to support learning in a variety of settings other than the classroom	Learning about and taking advantage of opportunities to support children's efforts to learn or study outside of the classroom
Expanding Community Development	
Involving the school in planning and decision-making as a community institution, as well as creating opportunities for community support groups to use the school's resources to help meet the students and their families	Participating in and supporting efforts to ensure that community planning and decision-making groups consider educational issues in their work as well as helping the wider community learn about and draw on school resources that can help support students and their families

This chart is adapted from materials created by the National Center for Family and Community Connections with Schools, Southwest Educational Development Laboratory (2006).

tive student as well as home-school outcomes (Brooks & Markman, 2005; Catambis, 2001; Fantuzzo et al., 2004; Haney & Hill, 2004; Hoover-Dempsey et al, 2005; Jeynes, 2005; Leibhaman et al., 2005). For example, a program that implements multiple strategies to increase communication between the school and home is likely to result in raised awareness of what students are doing in school and the importance of issues such as attendance, testing, school choice, and other options. Each school community—teachers, other school, staff, and family members—has to design a program and initiate the types of involvement that will best meet its goals.

A CULTURE OF CARING AND RESPECT

When a wide array of stakeholders come together and engage in meaningful interactions, the result is *synergy*—"the combined, or cooperative effects produced by the relationships among various forces, particles, elements, or parts or individuals in a given context—effects that are not otherwise possible" (Corning, 2003, p. 2). All of those involved—teachers, family members, students, or others engaged in the process—become jointly responsible for the education of children in the school community. These efforts engage teachers and family members in the "critical and serious work of rethinking educational structures and practices" (Fine, 1993, pp. 682–683). Epstein's model (2001) is the direct opposite of the one-way approach common to traditional programs described earlier (See Figure 2.1). Instead, its multidirectional communication allows the interests, needs, efforts, and plans of those involved—the natural "overlapping spheres of influence" (Epstein, 2001, p. 76)—to drive the actions and design of the program. It fosters respect and caring and allows all those involved—family members, community members, students, and teachers—to draw on the strengths of a variety of talents and experience to meet student needs.

The creation of these relationships rests heavily on the teachers' efforts to surface and address issues related to the adult family members including:

1. definition of an appropriate educational role,
2. beliefs about appropriate methods for child rearing,
3. feelings about their ability to help children based on their skills and knowledge level,
4. beliefs about their ability to teach children,
5. access to other resources for needed assistance, and
6. feelings of being welcomed and invited to the school (Henderson & Mapp, 2002).

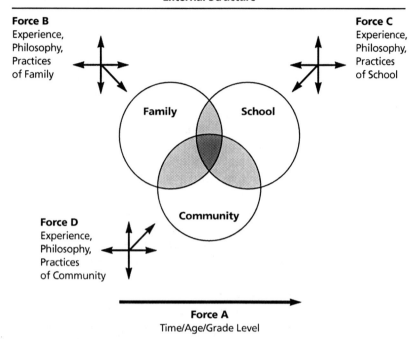

Figure 2.1.   Epstein's model of overlapping spheres of influence of family, school, and community on children's learning.

There are common practices found in research on effective family involvement efforts that can help teachers create a receptive culture that fosters increased and meaningful involvement for families of students representing diverse populations (Ferguson, 2005a):

- *Create activities that focus directly on specific classroom needs*—Often when we take a generic approach to increasing family involvement, we fail to address issues that are unique to the school community and the students specifically. All family members need help to navigate the educational system. Teachers can conduct workshop-type meetings with families to help build their understanding of how schools work and what's expected of both families and students. If families are limited by transportation, we can hold these meetings close to work places and at times that align to the adult work schedules.
- *Adopt a collaborative model that encourages and allows everyone to participate*—During the first stages of these efforts, the differences between teachers and student families may seem too large to bridge, but repeated interactions will build shared understanding. With shared

understanding, these differences become the "synergy" Corning (2003) that support effective programs. Teachers who engage in parents-as-teachers programs find that they can learn valuable information from the parents of their students, not only about the students themselves, but also about their methods of communicating with parents. These types of interactions can provide opportunities to surface and address issues related to family beliefs about education and their ability to support student learning.

- *Make outreach a priority*—In the highly demanding environment in which teachers work, it is often hard for them to reach out to parents. However, research clearly finds that when we take the time to reach actively out to parents through multiple strategies that make it possible for families to get involved at school, as well as at home, our efforts will be more effective. The key to this strategy is not to increase the teacher's workload, but to involve family and community members in a variety of ways in order to spread the tasks across many shoulders rather than a few. A common strategy for this is a communication "tree."

- *Recognize that developing relationships and trust takes time*—Building relationships often requires multiple interactions through a variety of sources. Teachers and families sometimes lose momentum when relationship building stalls—as it often will—particularly if there is wide divergence among the participants' cultural backgrounds. However, the far-reaching impact of meaningful relationships on the viability and quality of these efforts makes the time and energy worthwhile.

CONCLUSION

Redding, Langdon, Meyer, and Sheley (2004) describe effective family involvement programs as having a "greater reservoir of trust and respect, increased social capital for children, and a school community more supportive of each child's school success (p. 6)." These words define the goal of all of those who support active family involvement in their children's education. There is no formula for achieving this goal, and the innate contextual factors within a school community make teacher-family connections a complex process. When we actively reach out and engage family members, we can create stronger educational support systems. The first step in this process is exploring the perspectives of those involved—teachers and families. With time, all of those involved will develop caring and respectful relationships that foster collaborative interactions that result in additional support for student learning as well as support for families in their efforts to support their children's learning.

QUESTIONS

As teachers begin or continue their efforts to engage student families in support classroom learning, the following questions can help to raise issues of importance:

1. What existing programs or activities foster interactions among all stakeholders?
2. How effective are these efforts?
3. How do you know they are effective?
4. How do teachers learn about the contextual factors that impact the education of children in their classrooms?
5. How often and what activities take the teachers out of the classroom and into the community to engage with families?
6. What strategies do teachers use to make families feel welcome?
7. How do teachers address issues related to language?
8. What actions are taken to anticipate and address factors that inhibit family participation?
9. What actions are taken that provide families with an opportunity to build and foster networks that support relationship building as well support for student achievement?
10. How do teachers provide opportunities for *listening* to the concerns and ideas of family members?
11. How do teachers engage family members in efforts to identify areas of need—information and support—and determine how to addresses these areas of need?

REFERENCES

Adler, S. M. (2004). Home-school relations and the construction of racial and ethnic identity of Hmong elementary students. *The School Community Journal, 14*(2), 57–75.

Birch, T. C., & Ferrin, S. E. (2002). Mexican American parental participation in public education in an isolated Rocky Mountain rural community. *Equity & Excellence in Education, 35*(1), 70–78. EJ646575.

Boethel, M. (2002). *Readiness: School, family, and community connections.* Austin, TX: Southwest Educational Development Laboratory.

Boethel, M. (2003). *Diversity: School, family, and community connections.* Austin, TX: Southwest Educational Development Laboratory.

Brooks-Gunn, J., & Markman, L. B. (2005). The contribution of parenting to ethnic and racial gaps in school readiness. *Future of Children, 15*(1), 139–168.

Catambis, S. (2001). Expanding knowledge of parental involvement in children's secondary education: Connections with high school senior's academic success. *Social Psychology of Education, 5,* 149–177.

Chrispeels, J. H., & Rivero, E. (2001). Engaging Latino families for student success: How parent education can reshape parents' sense of place in the education of their children. Peabody *Journal of Education, 76*(2), 119–169. EJ654790.

Collignon, F. F., Men, M., & Tan, S. (2001). Finding ways in: Community-based perspectives on Southeast Asian family involvement with schools in a New England state. *Journal of Education for Students Placed at Risk, 6*(1&2), 27–44.

Cooper, C. W., & Christie, C. A. (2005). Evaluating parent empowerment: A look at the potential of social justice evaluation in education. *Teachers College Record, 107*(10), 2248–2274.

Corning, P. (2003). *Nature's magic: Synergy in evolution and the fate of humankind.* New York: Cambridge University Press.

Dearing, E., McCartney, K., Weiss, H. B., Kreider, H., & Simpkins, S. (2004). The promotive effects of family educational involvement for low-income children's literacy. *Journal of School Psychology, 42,* 445–460.

Desimone, L., Finn-Stevenson, M., & Henrich, C. (2000). Whole school reform in a low-income African American community: The effects of the CoZi Model on teachers, parents, and students. *Urban Education, 35*(3), 269–323. EJ612404.

Elbaz, F. (1991). Research on teachers' knowledge. *Journal of Curriculum Studies, 23,* 1–19.

Elliot, A., & Drake, S. M. (1999, April). *Concentric storying: A vehicle for professional development in teacher education.* Paper presented at American Educational Research Association Annual Meeting in Montreal Canada.

Epstein, J. L. (2001). *School, family, and community partnerships: Preparing educators and improving schools.* Boulder, CO: Westview Press.

Fan, X. (2001). Parental involvement and students' academic achievement: A growth modeling analysis. *The Journal of Experimental Education, 70*(1), 27–61. EJ642228.

Fantuzzo, J., McWayne, C., & Perry, M. (2004). Multiple dimensions of family involvement and their relations to behavioral and learning competencies for urban, low-income children. *The School Psychology Review, 33*(4), 467–480.

Ferguson, C. (2004). *Learning from Their Words and Actions: Using Narrative Studies to Develop a Framework for Defining Actualized Best Practices.* Paper presented at the American Educational Research Association Annual Meeting.

Ferguson, C. (2005a, August). *Organizing family and community connections with schools: How do school staff build meaningful relationships with all stakeholders?* (A Research Strategy Brief). Austin, TX: Southwest Educational Development Laboratory.

Ferguson, C. (2005b, September). *Reaching out to diverse populations: What can schools do to foster family-school connections.* (A Research Strategy Brief). Austin, TX: Southwest Educational Development Laboratory.

Ferguson, C. (2006). *Beyond the Building: A facilitation guide for school, family and community connections.* Austin, TX: Southwest Educational Development Laboratory.

Fine, M. (1993). [Ap]parent involvement: Reflection on parents, power, and urban public schools. *Teachers College Record, 94*(4).

Goldenberg, C., Gallimore, R., Reese, L., & Garnier, H. (2001). Cause or effect? A longitudinal study of immigrant Latino parents' aspirations and expectations of their children's school performance. *American Educational Research Journal, 38*(3), 547–582.

González, N., & Moll, L. C. (2002). Cruzando el Puente: Building bridges to funds of knowledge. *Educational Policy, 16*(4), 623–641.

Greenfield, P. M., Quiroz, B., &. Raeff, C. (2000). Cross-cultural conflict and harmony in the social construction of the child. In S. Harkness, C. Raeff, & C. R. Super (Eds.), *The social construction of the child: The nature of variability. New Directions in child development.* San Francisco: Jossey-Bass.

Hall, N., & Sham, S. (1998). *Language brokering by Chinese children.* Paper presented at Annual Conference of the British Educational Research Association, Dublin, Ireland.

Hamachek, D. (1999). Effective teachers: What they do, how they do it, and the importance of self-knowledge. In R. P Lipka & T. M. Brinthaupt (Eds.), *The role of self in teacher development* (pp. 189–224). Albany: State University of New York Press.

Haney, M. H., & Hill, J. (2004). Relationships between parent-teaching activities and emergent literacy in preschool children. *Early Child Development and Care, 17*(3), 215–228.

Henderson, A. & Mapp, K. (2002). *A new wave of evidence: The impact of school, family, and community connections on student achievement.* Austin, TX: Southwest Educational Development Laboratory.

Hoover-Dempsey, K. V., & Sandler, H. M. (2005). Final Performance Report for OERI Grant # R305T010673: *The Social Context of Parental Involvement: A Path to Enhanced Achievement.* Presented to Project Monitor, Institute of Education Sciences, U.S. Department of Education, March 22, 2005.

Jeynes, W. H. (2005). Research digest: Parental involvement and student achievement: A meta-analysis. *Research Digest,* Harvard Family Research Project. Retrieved from, http://www.gse. harvard.edu/hfrp/projects/fine/resources/digest/meta.html

Johnstone, T. R., & Hiatt, D. B. (1997). *Development of a school-based parent center for low income new immigrants.* Paper presented at the annual meeting of the American Educational Research Association, Chicago, IL. (Eric Document Reproduction Service No. ED407156.76).

Jordan, C, Orozco, E., Averett, A., & Buttram, J. (2001*). Emerging issues in school, family, and community connections.* Austin, TX: Southwest Educational Development Laboratory.

Leibhaman, M. E., Alexander, J. M., Johnson, K. E., Neitzel, C. L., & Reis-Henrie, F. P. (2005). Parenting behaviors associated with the maintenance of preschoolers' interests: A prospective longitudinal study. *Applied Developmental Psychology, 26*(4), 397–414.

Levine, E. B., & Trickett, E. J. (2000). Toward a model of Latino parent advocacy for educational change. *Journal of Prevention & Intervention in the Community, 20*(1/2), 121–137.

López, G. R. (2001). *On whose terms? Understanding involvement through the eyes of migrant parents.* Paper presented at the Annual Meeting of the American Educational Research Association, Seattle, WA.

Mayher, J. S. (1990). *Uncommon sense: Theoretical practice in language education.* Portsmouth, NH: Boynton/Cook.

McLoyd, V. C., Hill, N. E., & Dodge, K. A. (2005). *American family life: ecological and cultural diversity.* New York: Guilford Press.

Meyer, R. J. (1999). Spiders, rats, and transformation. *Primary Voices K–6: Transforming Our Teacher and Learning, 8*(2), 3–9.

Moll, L. C., & Greenberg, J. B. (1990). Creating zones of possibilities: Combining social contexts for instruction. In L. C. Moll's *Vygotsky and education: Instructional implications and applications of sociohistorical psychology* (pp. 314–348). New York: Cambridge University Press.

Musti-Roa. S., & Cartledge, G. (2004). Making home an advantage in the prevention of reading failure: Strategies for collaborating with parents in urban schools. *Preventing School Failure, 48*(4), 15–21.

Paratore, J. R. (2006). Approaches to family literacy: Exploring possibilities. *Reading Teacher, 59*(4), 394–396.

Paratore, J. R., Melzi, G., & Krol-Sinclair, B. (1999). *What should we expect of family literacy? Experiences of Latino children whose parents participate in an intergenerational literacy project.* Newark, DE: International Reading Association. (Eric Document Reproduction Service No. ED436759).

Pena, D. C. (2000). Parent involvement: Influencing factors and implications. *The Journal of Educational Research, 94*(1), 42–54.

Redding, S., Langdon, J., Meyer, J., & Sheley, P. (April, 2004). *The effects of comprehensive parent engagement on student learning outcomes.* Paper presented at the annual meeting of the American Educational Research Association, San Diego, CA.

Reese, L., & Gallimore, R. (2000). Immigrant Latinos' cultural model of literacy development: An evolving perspective on home-school discontinuities. *American Journal of Education, 108*(2), 103–134. EJ624173.

Rimm-Kaufman, S. E., Pianta, R. C., Cox, M. J., & Bradley, R. H. (2003). Teacher-rated family involvement and children's social and academic outcomes in kindergarten. *Early Education & Development, 14*(2), 179–198.

Rodriguez-Brown, F. V., Fen Li, R., & Albom, J. B. (1999). Hispanic parents' awareness and use of literacy-rich environments at home and in the community. *Education and Urban Society, 32*(1), 41–58.

Sanders, M. G. (2000). Creating successful school-based partnership programs with families of special needs students. *The School Community Journal, 10*(2), 37–56.

Scribner, J. D., Young, M. D., & Pedroza, A. (1999). Building collaborative relationships with parents. In P. Reyes, J. D. Scribner & A. Paredes-Scribner (Eds.), *Lessons from high-performing Hispanic schools: Creating learning communities* (pp. 36–60). New York, NY: Teachers College Press.

Smrekar, C., & Cohen-Vogel, L. (2001). *March toward excellence: School success and minority student achievement in Department of Defense schools.* Report presented at the National Educational Goals Panel, Washington DC.

Suárez-Orozco, C., & Suárez-Orozco, M. M. (2001). Immigrant children and the American Project. *Education Week, 20*(27), 56.

Swick, K. J. (2003). Communication concepts for strengthening family-school-community partnerships. *Early Childhood Education Journal, 30*(4), 275–280.

Todd, E. S., & Higgins, S. (1998). Powerlessness in professional and parent relationships. *British Journal of Sociology of Education, 19*(2), 227–236.

Vasquez, O., Pease-Alvarez, L., & Shannon, S.M. (1994). *Pushing boundaries: Language and culture in a Mexicano community.* New York: Cambridge University Press.

CHAPTER 3

DEVELOPING AN UNDERSTANDING OF FAMILIES AND THE COMMUNITY

Reyna García Ramos

COMMUNITY PROFILE

With great enthusiasm, Tom brought a box of his favorite dessert to his first parent meeting. During the meeting he noted that the parents did not choose his dessert. He felt disappointed. However, later he observed that the parents selected local food brought by other parents to this meeting. After the meeting, Tom strolled along the main street noting the kinds of foods displayed in the window and planned local choices for the next meeting.

Toward an Understanding of the Community

Traditional ways of reaching out to parents have not helped increase parent participation. As the faces of parents change, then so should the ways in which we conceptualize parent involvement and home-school connections. Even though traditional concepts about parent involvement con-

Promising Practices for Teachers to Engage Families of English Language Learners, pages 33–41
Copyright © 2007 by Information Age Publishing
All rights of reproduction in any form reserved.

tinue to persist (Lee & Bowen, 2006) it is imperative that schools begin to change their understanding of parents, their roles in the education of their children and ways to build lasting connections that impact families in the future. As new parents come into the school, it is essential that they too be afforded the kinds of opportunities that pervious parents have had to shape the schools' understanding about parents and the community. As the demographics in the community change, then too does the need to continuously revise instruments such as the community profile. Finally, as the English language learner (ELL) population continues to rise, schools will benefit from utilizing the above steps to ensure that they are reaching out to their most disenfranchised population in ways that will positively impact the lives of children and the lives of families in the community.

Teachers can help create positive lines of communication by becoming informed about the school and its surrounding community. Often, teachers are at a loss for understanding the school community and locating resources available to students and their families. As teachers prepare for the start of the academic year, ensuring for successful parent-connections can be accomplished with careful preparation and planning. Teachers, in essence, may be able to break down any barriers that have existed in the past by developing an understanding of the community and students' life (Banks et al., 2005). A community profile, therefore allows teachers to view the school and its surrounding area through eyes of students and parents.

A community profile is not a one-page sheet with fact and data about the community and its resources, but an opportunity for teachers to develop the skills they need to interact with parents. Often teachers avoid interactions with parents since they never learned how to interact with them in the first place (McGee Banks, 2003). Most cities and schools publish lists of community resources (libraries, medical clinics, elected officials, fire departments, poison control, etc.) but few publish these lists in the various languages that are represented in the community and with listings that are important for the families.

Orellana and Hernández (1999) suggest that teachers get out into the community with their students and take *community-based literacy walks*. Community-based literacy walks afford teachers the opportunity to understand places that are important to their students and their parents. During such a walk, teachers will perceive the community through the eyes of students. Literacy walks afford teachers and schools the opportunity to note community landmarks and places that are less known to the establishment but may be invaluable to the survival of local families. An example of this is discovering newspapers and ads on display in shops and local meeting places and the availability of neighborhood libraries and internet resources can shed light on sources of print and other literacy resources available to children and families. These walks can also generate a connection to a community that often feels distant to teachers.

Getting Started

Whether in an elementary or secondary school setting, teachers can take several steps to create a community-based literacy walk that will yield a "community map" (O'Sullivan, 2001). This can help inform the knowledge that teachers have about the community and the resources that parents can access.

1. First, an actual map that shows the route around the perimeter of the school will allow the teacher to make a brief sketch of the route that the students and teacher are to take. Depending on grade level, teachers can separate students into groups and then assign them to parent leaders. This leads us to the next point.

2. The construction of a profile is a great opportunity to invite parents into the classroom to assist in the process and the construction of the final product. Parents can be additional supervision for small students, or they can be guides for students at the upper elementary and secondary levels. The more parents are informed about the activity and its goals, the more parents will want to participate to ensure that its success.

3. Students should work in teams. Assigning students to teams and utilize cooperative learning strategies (Calderon, 1989).

4. Students will need several materials to make this profile a reality. Paper, pencil or pen, a disposable camera, or drawing paper.

5. Finally, some preparation for students is essential. Students need to understand that they are part of the success of this walk, and they need to keep a watchful eye during this walk and record their observations. Their observations notes can be part of future journal writing experience in the classroom or an ethnographic project of secondary students. Valuable opportunities for instructional materials can evolve out of this assignment that can enhance learning during social studies, history and the language-arts curriculum.

O'Sullivan (2001) has further suggested that teachers can benefit from "community mapping" which allow teachers and students ways to each notice what the other has missed on their daily trips to a school campus. Mapping is also a way for teachers to create an "awareness" of the community. In this way, limit the generalizations that often lead to stereotypes that are developed from lack of specific knowledge about families (Cazden & Mehan, 1989).

TABLE 3.1
Questions and Writing Prompts for the Community-Walk According to School Levels

Elementary	Secondary
Which direction is your home?	Which direction is your home? • Distance • Direction (east, west, north, south)
How do you get to school?	How do you get to school? • Route • Length of time
What do you see on your way to school?	What do you see on your way to school? • Businesses • Homes • Parks • People • Traffic
What do you see on your way home from school?	What do you see on your way home from school? How is it different then what you see in the morning? • Businesses • Homes • Parks • People • Traffic
Count the signs or billboard you see on this walk?	Count the signs or billboard you see on this walk?

What do the signs say?	What do the signs say?
	• How many different categories?
	  a. Advertising
	  b. Announcements
	  c. Political

Where do you see words?	Where do you see print? • What kind of print? •
Where do you see numbers?	Where do you see numbers?
Other observations • •	Other observations • •

Note: The above prompts are to help teachers get started. The template can easily be connected to the History and Social Studies framework for the California Department of Education for all grade levels.

When a community-based literacy walk is conducted early in the beginning of the academic year, it will allow students and teacher to speak about
a community in familiar terms. The outcome of this effort allows the
teacher to come up with a list of community resources that can enhance a
traditional list of community resources; it also now has a narrative of a community and its history. The narrative that emerges will help new teachers to
understand parents in the context of larger social networks. It will also give
teachers factual knowledge to use as part of bridging the discourse gap
between ELL parents and the schools. Now back to school night, parent
conferences and other school-parent events allow both teachers and parents to use common cultural knowledge and language that grew out of an
understanding of a community and its needs. Moll (1988) contends that
existing practices underestimate and constrain what Latino and other children are able to learn and to do. He suggests that the secret to successful
learning, particularly literacy-related, is for schools to investigate and tap
into the "hidden" home and community resources of their students.

Sending the profile home to parents to add or make changes to the profile is a way for parents to have input into the process. A *parent co-construct*
community profile turns into a list of resources that includes where parents
shop, places parents most often frequent and where they go for relevant
information (local market, bakeries, Spanish radio station and others). Parents' voice into the construction of a community profile adds further validity
to the profile. It becomes one that has value for teachers and parents alike.
This process would legitimize the "funds of knowledge" that parents hold
about the world in which they live (Moll, Amanti, Neff, & Gonzalez, 1992).
The outcome of such efforts go a long way to create an inviting environment
that parents look for as they contemplate participation in the school and
school related activities, especially if parents are trying to understand a
school system in a language they have not dominated in the past.

It is important to help parents understand what is expected of them and
to help facilitate their involvement. If parents receive assistance they are
looking for from teachers they will develop a bond with them that will last
long after their children have moved on from their classroom. Establishing
positive relationships with parents will also help prompt parents to take the
initiative on subsequent projects and in the coming years. Capacity building is important for the success of the students, parents, school and the
community.

SCHOOL TOUR

Rosalía, a young mother of 3, was sending her oldest off to kindergarten for
the first time. She had just moved and did not know anyone. She found the

local elementary school by asking others in her apartment complex the location of the school. Her kindergartener (Jessie) was very anxious about his first day at school. This was Jessie's first schooling experience, and it was in English. That morning, Rosalía went to Ms. Hernandez, the teacher, to ask what she should do to help ease Jessie's anxiety as he was on the verge of tears. Although, Ms. Hernandez let parents stay for the first hour to reassure the children but were later asked to leave. Ms. Hernandez informed parents that the kindergartens would be taken on a tour of the campus to familiarize them with the nurse's office, the principal's office, the cafeteria, and where to wait for parents after school. Rosalía lamented that she had not been invited go on the tour, for she too wanted to know the layout of this school.

The above vignette is an example of a common experience for parents and children with public schools, especially immigrant families (Suarez-Orozco & Suarez-Orozco, 2001). This expresses 5-year-old Jessie's troubling experiences on his first day of class. Ms. Hernandez could have used the tour offered to her class as a way to also orient the parents of her students. This tour could have been used as a way to orient Jessie's younger siblings, as his sister ended up in the same class a year later. There are techniques that teachers use in class that are effective for their students and with a little elaboration and careful planning, can also be used with parents as well.

Parents are just as anxious about the first day of school as their children. "Where is my daughter's classroom?" "How far does my son need to walk to get to the bathroom?" "Where is the office in relation to the playground?" ELL parents not only have the same questions, but also often are at a loss of whom to ask for the answers. Teachers can do much to help introduce ELL parents to the school by organizing a campus tour in which parents will get to meet key individuals throughout the school. If students are new to the school, then so are their parents. Just as the students need to find their way around the school, so will the parents. Taking students on a school tour also allows teachers to know who is familiar with the school, returning students, and who is new to the school (Murray, 2002).

Being familiar with the campus is not only essential for establishing a student's comfort level, but it is also a way to help promote school safety and awareness on the layout of the school. A school tour should include opportunities to meet key people on campus. Some of the most obvious persons that parents should meet are the principal, the PTA president, parent liaison, and anyone else that can help orient parents. A teacher can schedule an on-campus tour for her students and their parents before the start of the academic year. Working parents find it difficult to come onto campus during the middle of the day, so it is better to organize a campus tour the Saturday before the start of the school year or the morning school begins, in the hours prior to the beginning of class.

In either case, teachers should possess essential information regarding the students in her class, which students are new students to the school, and the students' home addresses. Invitations should be mailed home in the multiple languages that students represent. The invitation should include a map of the school and a list of who will be available to greet parents on the tour. Ideally, this is a great opportunity for new parents, but returning parents to the school will also enjoy meeting the new teacher and any changes in personnel that have occurred over the summer. This is a great opportunity for teachers to team up with other teachers at the same grade level so that the tour becomes a team effort. It is especially important that established teachers team up with new teachers to provide them with practice in strategies that reach out to parents.

Key people, like the principal, are critical and the sooner parents understand roles of key persons on campus, the better they will be at deciphering how to address concerns they may have about their child's needs. This provides an ideal opportunity for parents to find out about the roles of the personnel they meet and inquire about opportunities for participation in their child's classroom. Although ideally this should be a school effort, other faculty and the administration will realize how easily a school tour can be organized. Most important, others will notice how much is accomplished in an event that gives parents an orientation at the beginning of the academic year prior to back-to-school night.

COMMUNITY SCHOOL FAIR

Some schools have organized a school fair the weekend before the start of the academic calendar (Wiltz, 2004). The fair invites all parents to come out and meet the teachers, administration, and staff. A school fair can host community agencies and social service agencies to come share information with parents and students. During the school fair, school tours are arranged to occur throughout the event. Now parents can have referential knowledge about where on campus to meet or how to help ease their child's anxiety about entering a new school. This event ensures that the academic year will be off to a good start. A new student can meet his teachers; new parents can get familiar with the school. A school fair would need to be school wide; a school-tour, however, can be for your classroom only.

CONCLUDING REMARKS

The educational community has long been concerned about the future of language minority students. Language minority students face many challenges in academic outcomes due to ELL status, lack of educational resources and a growing emphasis on high stakes testing (Campbell, 2004; Nieto, 2004). Research indicates that language and ethnic minority students do not fare as well as Anglo and mainstream students. While a radical restructuring of the school systems is needed in order to address the needs of today's student (Campbell, 2004; Valencia, 1991), more emphasis has focused on the need to establish home-school connections (Lee & Bowen, 2006) that help language and ethnic minority students and their parents succeed in K–12 educational settings.

Reaching out toward ELL parents is especially crucial as many ELL parents are not only learning about a new school but also learning how to "do" schooling in another language (Adler, 2004; Suarez-Orozco & Suarez-Orozco, 2001). Home-School connections have traditionally worked under an outdated concept of parent involvement that was developed when the United States had a more homogenous orientation about schooling (McGee Banks, 2003). Now, however, schools need to adopt patterns of parent connections that reflect the realities of parents' today, particularly ELL parents. Given the research indicating that parents play a critical role in their children's academic success (Lee & Bowen, 2006); it is important that teachers create strategies that help develop connections with ELL parents. This chapter examines how a community profile and a school tour can help teachers establish positive communication lines between parents and the classroom.

QUESTIONS TO HELP STIMULATE DISCUSSION AND THOUGHTFUL PLANNING

1. What have you done to reach out to ELL parents?
2. What are traditional models of parent-involvement that exists on your campus? How would they need to be modified for ELL parents?
3. Take your own community-walk. What questions do you have about the community that would need to be answered before you take your class?
4. How would you plan a community-based literacy walk for your students?
5. How would you include parents in a school tour?

REFERENCES

Adler, S. M. (2004). Home-school relations and the construction of racial and ethnic identity of Hmong elementary students. *The School Community Journal, 14*(2), 57–75.

Banks, J., Cochran-Smith, M., Moll L., Richert, A., Zeichner, K., LePage, P., Darling-Hammond, L., & Duffy, H. (2005). Teaching diverse learners. In L. Darling-Hammond & J. Bransford (Eds.), *Preparing teachers for a changing world* (pp. 232–274). San Francisco: Wiley & Sons.

Calderón, M. (1989, September). Cooperative learning for LEP students. *Intercultural Development Research Association Newsletter, 16*(9) 1–7.

Cazden, C., & Mehan, H. (1989). Principles form sociology and anthropology. In M. C. Reynolds (Ed.), *Knowledge base for the beginning teacher* (pp. 47–57). New York: Pergamon Press.

Carroll, T. G., Fulton, K., Abercrombie, K., & Yoon, I. (2004). *Fifty years after Brown v. Board of Education: A two-tiered education system.* Washington, DC: National Commission on Teaching and America's Future.

Campbell, D. E. (2004). *Choosing democracy: A practical guide to multicultural education* (3rd ed). Upper Saddle River, NJ: Prentice-Hall.

Lee, J-S., & Bowen, N. K. (2006). Parent involvement, cultural capital, and the achievement gap among elementary school children. *American Educational Research Journal, 43*, 193–218.

McGee Banks, C. (2003). Families and teachers working together for school improvement. In J. A. Banks & C. A. McGee Banks (Eds.), *Multicultural education: Issues & perspectives* (pp. 402–420). New York: Wiley & Sons.

Moll, L. (1988). Some key issues in teaching Latino students. *Language Arts, 65*, 465–472.

Moll, L. C., Amanti, C., Neff, D., & Gonzalez, N. (1992). Funds of knowledge for teaching: A qualitative approach to connect households and classrooms. *Theory into Practice, 31*, 132–141.

Murray, B. P. (2002). *The new teacher's complete sourcebook: Grades K–4.* New York: Scholastics.

Nieto, S. (2004). *Affirming diversity: The sociopolitical context of multicultural education* (4th ed.). White Plains, NY: Longman.

Orellana, M. F., & Hernández, A. (1999). Talking the walk: Children reading urban environmental print. *The Reading Teacher, 56*, 612–619.

O'Sullivan, M. (2001). *Community awareness and community-mapping.* Knoxville, TN: The Urban Summer Institute.

Scribner, J. D., Young, M. D., & Pedroza, A. (1999). Building collaborative relationships with parents. In P. Reyes, J. D. Scribner, & A. Paredes Scribner (Eds.), *Lessons form high-performing Hispanic schools: Creating learning communities* (pp. 36–60). New York: Teachers College Press.

Suárez-Orozco, C., & Suárez-Orozco, M. M. (2001). Children of Immigration. Cambridge, MA: Harvard University Press.

Valencia, R. R. (1991). The plight of Chicano students: An overview of schooling conditions and outcomes. In R. R. Valencia (Ed.), *Chicano school failure and success: Research and policy agendas for the 1990s* (pp. 3–26). New York: The Falmer Press.

Wiltz, S. M. (2004). Brining Parents on Board: Building strong home-school connections with immigrant families. In M. Sadowski (Ed.), *Teaching immigrant and second-language students: Strategies for success* (pp. 95–105). Cambridge, MA: Harvard Education Press.

CHAPTER 4

REACHING OUT
FROM THE CLASSROOM
TO THE FAMILIES

Diana B. Hiatt-Michael and Linda Purrington

During student teaching, Donielle observed how fearful students seemed to be on the first day of school, often clinging to parents or friends. Once in her own classroom, Donielle asked the principal if she could invite students and their parents before school opened. To her amazement, almost all of Donielle's new students along with family members attended her small "open house" and bonded as a classroom family because of that experience.

PARENT COMMUNICATION BEFORE THE CLASSROOM
DOOR OFFICIALLY OPENS

Hosting Open Houses/Open Classrooms

Events to forge relationships between your classroom and home should not wait until the school doors officially open. Hosting an open house in your classroom before the beginning of the year affords a relaxed and informal opportunity to become acquainted with your students and their families. Such an event will lay the foundation for respectful and trusting relationships, a connection that Moll and Arnot-Hopffer's (2005) research

Promising Practices for Teachers to Engage Families of English Language Learners, pages 43–60
Copyright © 2007 by Information Age Publishing
All rights of reproduction in any form reserved.

indicates is strongly lacking between teachers and parents of English language learners (ELL) students. During this informal social setting, teachers may establish a friendly and nonthreatening climate for the coming year (Foster, 1994). Teacher, the students, and their family members will exchange important information and useful to cross-cultural barriers and information to build positive working relationships (Chavkin, 1993).

Many schools, recognizing the rewards of an open house before classes begin, make such programs a school wide effort (Education World, 2003). In addition to showcasing classrooms, school wide open houses provide students and families with an introduction to school facilities and total campus. At the same time, families may be introduced to school programs, school organizations, community support organizations, school administration, special assignment faculty, and support staff. To encourage a sense of cultural comfort for ELL families, schools incorporate their cultural norms in this open house. For example, in a primarily Asian culture, the principal, as highest ranking person, begins the Open House in respect for the norms of their culture. In Providence, Rhode Island, veteran families are paired with new families so that veterans help newcomers join the school network of families (The "Met," personal communication, May, 2001).

As a new teacher, you may have the good fortune of joining a school that provides a "before school open house." If you do not, you can still seize the opportunity to conduct your own classroom open house and, later in collaboration with colleagues, promote the development of a schoolwide event. The following is a brief description of a first-hand experience with a before school open house program at an elementary school (Purrington, 1998). Many of the students and their families spoke Spanish as their primary language.

At this "Before School Open House," a welcome open house marquis message greeted parents, family members, and students as they arrived at the school the week before scheduled classes. Upper grade students in brightly-colored T-shirts were stationed around the school entrance and parking lot to welcome and guide visitors. Colorful balloons marked classrooms, special event areas, and program information booths. Visitors were handed a color-coded map that corresponded to the balloon colors and "hello" name-tags.

Parent, Teacher Association (PTA) volunteers sponsored tables brimming with snacks and beverages. They mingled with parents, recruited new PTA members, and shared opportunities for parent involvement. A drawing of new PTA members was conducted throughout the day and free pizza coupons were awarded to those whose names were selected. The coupons were provided by a local business in support of this event. School clubs decorated the quad with tabletop posters advertising student programs.

A school bus was parked outside the kindergarten building and "new riders" were invited to meet the driver and tour the bus. The driver handed out bookmarks, stickers, and school pencils. The kindergarten playground had tricycles, wagons, jump ropes, balls, swings, slides, and other equipment for new students to experience. A classroom aide supervised student play.

Inside the classroom, the teacher greeted parents, families, and new students with friendly conversation and displays of curriculum and sample student projects. At one table, persons could sign up to be a classroom volunteer and for the parent–teacher fall conference. Brochures with the fall calendar and an invitation to Back to School Night were available for all participants. The teacher took the initiative to greet each visitor personally and to invite families to fill out a family information sheet that would help the teacher get to know the students and their families better. The information sheet invited parents to share information or questions regarding their child. While parents chatted with the teacher, new students had the opportunity to paint a picture, engage in a craft, and/or explore the classroom. Two upper grade students were at-hand to interact with and help supervise younger students.

A similar scenario took place in classrooms throughout the school and throughout the day. Parents, family members, and students dropped in as their schedules permitted. In classrooms where the teacher was not bilingual, a bilingual aide or parent volunteer was available to translate and help bridge relationships. All materials were provided in the primary language of the parents. The intent of the open house before school was to be welcoming, festive, informal, and informative.

After the open house, a new teacher remarked that her new ELL parents were so friendly and engaging; this was a similar finding reported by Kelty (1997) in her thesis. Given that she did not speak Spanish, the new teacher had assumed that their meeting would be somewhat awkward and there would exist a social distance between them. What occurred was quite the opposite. Parents, grandparents, sisters, brothers, aunts, and uncles were eager to communicate and chatted informally in Spanish and English. They helped to bridge whatever language gaps may have existed. The teacher found the parents to be generous in offering their time and support. She began the new school year feeling excited about close connection between her work in the classroom and the families of her children.

Open houses before school begins need not be schoolwide. They may begin with a single teacher and a single classroom. A secondary science teacher at a Los Angeles area high school invited parents to a Get Acquainted Through Science Evening. He sent postcard invitations to the parents of his freshman students to join him for dessert, coffee and get acquainted introductions. Some of the teacher's former science students helped him to create and label the postcard invitations, translated into several community languages. Several of the students and their parents that were bilingual also helped to make follow-up reminder phone calls. The teacher enlisted the help of a few PTA parents to organize the dessert/coffee. During this classroom preschool open house, the teacher created several get acquainted activities with a science theme. Parents and students participated together in these activities as a way to introduce his approach to science instruction. The former students also helped with the evening activities.

Home Visits

Home visits will provide one of the richest sources of information about students (Sturrock, 2006; Winter, 1995). Historical roots of home visits lie in the Social Reform era of 1870–1920 (Bhavnagni & Krolikowski, 2000). These early attempts at home visits were to ameliorate home conditions that led to achievement problems at school. Home visits by teachers may serve a similar purpose, such as those initially-mandated by Head Start. However, the *academic purpose* of teacher home visits is to empower family members and the teacher (PICO National Network Case Study, n.d.). The foundation for a classroom community is built with each visit.

The most advantageous time to make home visits is before or at the beginning of the school year. A home visit opens the path of communication between family and teacher. The home visit sends a signal to the home that the teacher is friendly and wants to work with them (Bell, 1996). Parental defensiveness, blame on teachers or withdrawal is ameliorated. Teachers come together with families to build trusting relationships, sharing the hopes and expectations that each has for the student. The information gleaned during this firsthand opportunity, viewing the student and the family at home, is foundational to curricular planning and personal understanding of students (Moles, 2000).

Hunt (2002), a secondary teacher of ELL, shares his initial attempt to become better acquainted with his students. He wanted his students and families "to see me struggling with their native language on their home turf" just as he noted that they struggled with English in the classroom. Hunt perceived how daunting speaking on the telephone in another language can be. Therefore, he contacted each family of his students by phone, asking for an opportunity to visit in his halting Spanish. Prior to the call, Hunt had prepared a script with possible options. Even with such preparation, the phone calls presented challenges. He proudly reported all families accepted his offer to visit, and only the day and time of the visit were the negotiated issues.

When Hunt arrived at the home, he shared samples of the student's school work as a way to connect with the family. In addition, Hunt wanted his students to take an active role in this interface. He requested that they introduce family members and serve as hosts. He noted that the students and parents were helpful and understanding whenever his use of the language exceeded his command of Spanish.

Hunt's action research exemplified the caveats provided by Moles (1999), a longtime government researcher in parent involvement. Moles recommends advance notification by phone (or mail), flexible scheduling, and inclusion of the student during the visit. In some cultures, a formal request may be expected. A letter prepared and sent to the home by the school principal may prepare the families for subsequent contact by the teacher. Home visits provide the opportunity for families and teachers to meet in a setting where the teachers and the family members are on an equal power basis and teachers are not perceived as having the institutional advantage of the school (PICO National Network Case Study, n.d.). As perceived in Hunt's action research on home visits, these visits create a strong personal connection between the teacher and the family.

Research findings of teacher home visits support increased student attendance, reduction of student reports of disruptive behavior, improved appropriate academic placement of students, higher homework completion, improved academic achievement and test scores, and level of parent involvement at the school (EMT Associates Inc., 2005; Houston Independent School District, 1997).

The Parent/Teacher Home Visit Project was formed in 1998 by a group of faith-based congregations in Sacramento, CA, and expanded to collaborate with many affiliated groups. The staff of this project provide resources for teacher home visits and training across the nation for teachers to make effective home visits (C. Rose, personal communication, April 4, 2006). Rose reports that face-to-face visits are a common way of doing business in many of the Latino and Asian communities served by the school district. The purpose of the project is to "challenge assumptions about the role of teachers and parent, break down barriers, and insure accountability for student success" (PICO National Network Case Study, n.d.). One Sacramento school reported 21 different languages spoken in the home; 69% of families were immigrants from Southeast Asia and 12% were immigrants from Mexico and Central America. Home visits provided a positive means to cross language and cultural barriers and improve academic achievement of students from these families.

Although the project shares many success stories, initially teachers expressed concerns about home visits to certain urban areas (Furger, 2005). In order to alleviate teacher' fears, teachers made such visits in pairs or with another member of the staff. Some teachers selected an interpreter or school nurse to join them on the home visit made during daylight hours. However, these teachers reported back that they were surprised that most of these homes were pleasant and did not fit their prior mental images of inner city dwellings.

Home visits afford unique opportunities for teachers to observe the living arrangements, parenting practices, and family life. During a home visit, one teacher noted that the student's family of three lived in one large room with separate bath and kitchen area. The television and couch assumed a central position in the living area. Adjacent renters, apparently extended families, easily moved from one home to the next. Arousing music and animated voices dominated the air space. Throughout the visit, several adults reminded the student to perform certain tasks or behave in an appropriate manner. The teacher reflected how this living arrangement affected the student's capability to read or study.

Teachers share interesting ways to connect with the family during the visit. Dodd and Lilly (1997) describe the benefits to develop a family portfolio during the first home. The family portfolio may be a collection of teacher notes about the family, shared photographs, family history, photographs taken that day, a CD with favorite music, medical information, and anything that teacher and family want to include in the portfolio. The portfolio becomes the family's gift to the teacher. Depending on its contents, the teacher may exhibit all or portions of the portfolio in the classroom. This exhibition connects all the families in the classroom, developing a shared community with diverse family members. Others report that they took a family photograph and had those on the bulletin board to greet students on the first day of school.

However, many new and experienced teachers are reticent to make the trip into seemingly unknown territory (Taveras, 1998). Some teachers may be highly concerned that they alone cannot surmount the differences in culture and communication between themselves and the student families. In such situations, the teacher may select a well-established school parent to serve as a home visit partner. This parent becomes a coach, mentor, and ELL liaison for the teachers. Many schools have designated parent liaisons whose function is to support the teachers in home-school connections.

CONTINUED REACHING OUT THROUGHOUT THE YEAR: USE OF MULITPLE SOURCES OF COMMUNICATION

Overview

Parent communication refers to any one-way or two-way forms of communication between parents and the school including: informal conversations, formal meetings, presentations, conferences, special events, phone calls, newsletters, emails, notes, and websites. Parent involvement activities range from simple response to a note, to a weekly classroom newsletter or interactive classroom website.

The Students

Students are a major source of classroom-home communication (Hiatt-Michael, 2001). On a daily basis, a kindergarten teacher asked students to share one important thing that happened or something new that they learned at the end of the class. She reminded the students that their families wanted to hear what the child was doing and learning at school every day. Of course, not every comment reached the home, but the students acquired the skill to reflect on the day and often shared much more with family members. The tired "Nothing" response to "What happened in school today?" was changed to a healthy interchange of information on events.

Students continue to serve as a powerful source of home-school communication across the academic levels. Enthusiastic students express their news to their families. Disengaged students do not.

Notes to Parents

Across cultures, communication from the teacher—a person held in high regard—is valued (Hiatt-Michael, 2006). Unfortunately, parents expect that notes from teachers announce a problem with their child at school. To counteract that belief and expectation, teachers at all levels should develop an easy method to share good news with parents. With ELL families, short computer generated notes in the family's language may be handed to the elementary school child at the end of the day or sent via mail or e-mail to secondary school student families. Such pre-designed notes might read "A fine contribution in math class," "All homework was submitted on time this week," or "A kindness was observed today."

The pre-generated note does not have to describe the specific incident but encourages the child to provide the supporting details. Such a note will generate positive dialogue between school and home. A personal friend recently shared how much it meant to her and her daughter to receive a postcard from one of her high school teachers congratulating her on an assignment well done. They kept the postcard on their refrigerator and wrote a nice note back to the teacher. If a classroom aide or parent liaison who speaks the home language is available that person might create a short personal note.

Some teachers designate a specific day of the week for parents to expect regular communication from the teacher. Such communication may become a packet that contains personal notes with supporting work from the previous week as well as the weekly newsletter. For example, to prepare for the weekly parent communication, the teacher creates a set of hanging folders, one for each student in the class. Students as well as the teacher may place items into the folder. On the given day, all the items are placed in a colored packet, specially designed so that can be easily recognized by parents. These packets must be sturdy enough to withstand transport between school and home. At a middle school, the homeroom teacher sends home the student folders home every Thursday. The folders are bright blue with the school name and school mascot on the cover. All communications are printed in English and in the primary languages of the school's diverse families. Parents have shared that the routine and the folder help to make communication more regular and convenient.

Telephone Calls to Parents

Phone calls from the teacher can be useful to tell each parent of their child's progress and can be repeated as opportunities arise (Hiatt-Michael, 2001). Such calls counteract the feeling of many parents that schools only contact them when there is bad news. However, with ELL parents, the teacher should use the parents native language or request that a parent volunteer or parent liaison (see future section) make the phone call. Bittle (1975) cited the benefits to student learning when teachers provided parents with ideas for home learning activities and how to assist with homework. For example, the teacher or bilingual aide prerecords a daily or weekly message that can be accessed by all parents from their home or cell phones. A more contemporary approach is to utilize e-mail or a website. Cottle (1991) reports that such regular communication to middle-school parents increases school attendance and reduces student high school drop out rates.

Classroom Newsletter to Families

Newsletters provide an informative and inexpensive means to communicate with parents. School districts, schools, and individual classrooms publish parent newsletters. However, the newsletter that is most read is the classroom newsletter. Family members want to know what is happening in *their* child's classroom. Possible topics for inclusion encompass general items of information, school events, holidays and conferences, discipline policies, home activities parents can do with their children, and highlights of student or staff accomplishments. Moles (1999) recommends that the PTA, parent liaisons, teachers, and students be involved in the production of parent newsletters. Parents, teachers, administrators, and students may assist by providing articles or work. Newsletters should be available in the parents' primary language for parents who are not yet literate in their native language. Low-cost software packages are available for translation. The principal should have government funds to cover the cost of purchase so simply make a pleasant request. We promise you will be rewarded or contact us.

The director of a preschool parent literacy programs in California shared with colleagues that, at her child's school, the teacher sends home a Monday night newsletter. The director and other parents at the school expect that newsletter and plan the week according to the school activities. The day of the week does not matter. What matters is that the families are expecting the newsletter and its important information on the same day every week. In El Paso, Texas, Hueco Elementary School publishes a monthly newsletter for parents, but many teachers create a weekly or monthly newsletter (Funkhauser & Gonzales, 1998). In Irvine, California, student teachers work with their supervising teachers to prepare weekly parent newsletters. In our teacher education classes, we promote student editors of classroom and school newsletters to incorporate student thinking and writing into this form of home-school communication. Student participation promotes parental reading and a positive connection between classroom life and parenting.

Many schools utilize newsletters as a forum for parent surveys so two-way communication occurs between parents and the school (Decker & Majerczyk, 2000). Schools use newsletters as the medium to solicit family volunteers for the library or lunchroom, ensure sign-up for the teacher/father breakfast or grandparent's day, and request parent opinion regarding a proposed new school policy. Espinosa (1995) reported that Hispanic parents more frequently respond to such written communication (even in the families' native language) after direct personal contact and a relationship have been established.

A principal of a Chicago primary school asserted that newsletters grant equal access to all parents concerning school information (Allen-Jones, 2001). Newsletters, printed in representative languages of the school, secure that all families have the opportunity to receive school news. She stated that "newsletters provide information about the school and are essential to the home-school communication process."

A classroom newsletter created with input from the children should be developed and issued on a regular basis, preferably weekly (Allen-Jones, 2001). These newsletters can be reproduced in a consistent color and sent home on the same day of every week, making them easily recognizable to both children and parents. Parents anticipate these newsletters, brimming with information vital to the parents and their children. Classroom newsletters are regularly read by most parents and are more significant to families than the school newsletter. Student artwork and writing included in the newsletter reflect a child-centered philosophy, as well as provides interest. Personal notes in the classroom newsletter, such as recognizing parent volunteers or thanking parents for helping out with specific projects, create a sense of community as well as encourages additional involvement (Barbre & Hiatt-Michael, 2004).

Neighborhood Coffees

Neighborhood coffees can be organized jointly by teachers and parent volunteers to provide families of ELL with informal opportunities to talk with teachers and the school principal about issues related to their children (Moles, 1999). These informal gatherings can be held in homes, restaurants, senior citizen centers and other local community centers. They are usually well attended. Some parents feel more comfortable meeting there than in schools. These get-togethers are designed to give a small group of parents an informal opportunity to talk with school staff about issues affecting their children. For example, neighborhood coffees might be organized for parents of sixth-grade children who will soon be going to junior high to share ideas on helping them with this important transition.

An elementary school in Atlanta, Georgia, held neighborhood coffees the first Saturday morning of every month in a Mexican restaurant located in the families' neighborhood. The teachers and the bilingual liaison organized these meetings as a way to reach out to Latino parents whose children were bussed to a higher income school in the district. Through these coffees the families became more familiar with the school staff, and the staff had the opportunity to know the families' needs and concerns. After learning that the main barriers that prevented these families to participate in the school were lack of transportation, child care and language, the principal provided the families with these three resources (school bus, child care and translator) and the coffee meetings were moved to the school building (M. Gonzalez, personal communication, October, 2006).

BRIDGING HOME-SCHOOL RELATIONSHIPS
WITH BILINGUAL COMMUNITY LIAISONS

An unexpected family emergency caused fourteen-year-old Kinam to be absent from school for an extended period of time. Kinam's teacher, Breshna Fatari, had left a phone message in English inquiring about the girl's well-being but Kinam's parents spoke little English and were uncertain of how to navigate the school's electronic phone system to respond. They decided instead to write a note of explanation when they received a call from the school's bilingual liaison, Mrs. Avila. Mrs. Avila was able to communicate the circumstances of Kinam's absence to Breshna Fatari, coordinate a plan for Elena to make-up missed learning, and provide a resource for Kinam's parents in the event of a future emergency. Kinam's parents stopped by the school to thank Mrs. Avila in person and then to meet Breshna Fatari.

Most teachers understand that connecting with families yields positive results but they sometimes struggle with how to make the connection (Kyle, McIntryre, Miller, & Moore, 2002). Differences in culture, language, prior educational experiences, and time constraints present obstacles. Parent and community liaisons can help teachers bridge these obstacles and lead to very collaborative and rewarding partnerships (Bermudez & Padron, 1998). Many districts employ bilingual and multilingual parent and community liaisons to serve schools with large populations of ELL (Johnstone & Hiatt, 1997). Sometimes schools share these services and, in other instances, a liaison or liaisons are assigned to a single school. These liaisons are familiar with the school and community cultures and languages and truly serve to bridge communication and collaboration. They provide a valuable resource for classroom teachers to help build classroom and school communities of learners through collaboration among teachers, students, families, and community (McCaleb, 1997).

New teachers can find out about liaison services and schedules from their school administrators and administrative support staff. Parent and community liaisons support services may vary from district to district and school to school. Such services include: translation (written and oral), parent–teacher conference support, home visits, shared leadership and translation for parent meetings and parent programs, shared coordination of parent resources/support, parent workshops, and other services as needed to support home-school partnerships.

Some districts and schools hire bilingual instructional aides and/or bilingual program aides with shared responsibility for parent and community liaison services. These aides may spend a certain percent of their time working directly with students and/or designated programs. And/or, they may spend a designated amount of time providing parent and community liaison services. School administration and administrative support staff are the best source for finding out about aides' schedules and support services.

In the absence of or in addition to the sources above, classroom teachers may take the initiative to organize classroom parent and community volunteer support. Elementary teachers can take the first step by talking to their students' teachers from last year to find out which parents are bilingual and are able to volunteer their time and talent. New teachers can find out about their students' past teacher assignments from office administrative staff. When a parent or parents are not available within one class, it might be possible for a grade level team or several grade level teams to share and coordinate parent volunteer support services. Secondary teachers might coordinate these same efforts through their departments with the help of their department chairpersons.

A survey of school principals in California (Purrington, 2006) revealed an array of utilization of parent and community liaisons in schools. Some of the most common are identified in Table 4.1.

TABLE 4.1
How Parent/Community Liaisons May Assist the Teacher

Serve as newcomer student/family ambassadors
Support and initiate home visits
Co-lead parent meetings
Translate classroom newsletters into multiple languages
Translate notes sent home and phone calls to parents
Translate teacher/parent/student conferences
Translate and co-lead classroom and school meetings and events
Coordinate resources for parents
Organize phone trees and carpools
Tutor and mentor students and adults
Help with logistics, translation, and activities for Open Houses, Back-to-School Nights, Family Literacy/Math/Science Nights, special classroom/grade level/department programs and other special programs and events
Coordinate parent education programs
Coordinate parent volunteer services

COORDINATING WORK WITH FAMILIES AND STAFF WITH SCHOOL/DISTRICT POLICIES

Administrators are entrusted with the implementation of legal mandates, district guidelines, and policies emanating from various sources. Thus, whenever a new teacher is considering any innovative approach, such as preschool open house, home visits, or enlisting a parent liaison, the teacher should first consult with the site administrator. For example, parent and community liaison services are coordinated throughout the school and must adhere to school/district policy and guidelines. These policies and guidelines, such as those that protect individual confidentiality, must be obeyed by all teachers. Therefore, as a new teacher, you should personally acquire about the school policies and procedures before you retain or work with any parent and/or community liaison.

CONNECTION WITH FORMAL PARENT ASSOCIATIONS AND COUNCILS

Parent Teacher Association

The school's parent and teacher association may be another venue to locate parent and community liaison support. Parent and teacher associations sometimes provide volunteer support services and/or can point a teacher in the direction of someone(s) who can provide assistance. Parent and teacher associations may have a designated volunteer liaison or a committee of liaison volunteers that work closely with school administration, faculty, and staff to support home-school partnerships. Generally, parent teacher association contacts are posted on school websites, shared in newsletters, and available through school administration and administrative support staff.

Community Associations

In addition to parent volunteers, community organizations may be available to support home-school partnerships (Decker, Gregg, & Decker, 1996; Hiatt-Michael, 2003). For example, a local chapter of the American Association of University Women and Men (AAUW) and their members offer their commitment to serve in classrooms (AAUW, 2006). These AAUW volunteers arrived at the school on a weekly basis to support ELL in several classrooms. The AAUW volunteers became much more than tutors to the children and their families. The volunteers were viewed in some instances as second grandparents, mentors, and family friends. Certain volunteers attended student and family events and helped to coordinate resources and services. Volunteers worked closely with classroom teachers and school administration to coordinate efforts. New teachers may find out about community organization support through their school administration or by directly contacting community organizations to find out what they have to offer. The internet is a great source for community service group information as are local newspapers and local chamber of commerce groups.

Parent Advisory Committees

By law, public schools are required to involve all parents in the education of their child and there is an additional provision for parents of ELL (U.S. Department of Education, 2002a). Any school that has more than 21 students who are considered ELL and is receiving federal funds must have a bilingual advisory committee (U.S. Department of Education, 2002b). Members of this committee operate according to policies established by the district and at each school site. Fresno Unified School District's website presents a comprehensive plan (FUSD Master Plan for English Learners, 2006). Parents are elected to this committee and provide guidance to the school regarding the development, implementation, and evaluation of programs and parent involvement activities related to ELL.

Parents that participate on this committee are a vast resource for bridging relations with other parents and the community as a whole (Davies, Burch, & Johnson, 1992; Pena, 1998, 2000). These elected representatives from the community can help new teachers understand parent perspectives, concerns, and needs. They can connect new teachers to resources, including other parents, to help construct and support strong home-school partnerships. Also, bilingual advisory committee members are a sounding board for new ideas and new ways of involving and serving parents and community members in support of student learning and well-being.

Usually, the first fall meeting of each school's bilingual advisory committee is open to all parents and school members. Plan to attend so that parents observe that you are interested in their concerns and points of view. This meeting will give you a wealth of information. You are able to stand back and quietly note how the parents perceive the school, school staff, each other, the curriculum, school policies, and many other elements. This information will provide insights for your future work with them and others at the school. As you get to know your parents better, you may also encourage prospective parent leaders to also attend the bilingual advisory committee meetings to share their "voices" and to become more involved.

CREATING A PLAN TO REACH OUT TO PARENTS

In order to develop a manageable plan for parent involvement, the teacher should consider answering questions. The following (Table 4.2) is an

TABLE 4.2
Parent Communication Action Plan Goal

To introduce myself to students/parents/families and to learn more about students' backgrounds.

Objective	How will objective be completed?	Who will complete the objective?	When will objective be completed?
• Host open classroom during one morning and one afternoon before school begins. Invite students and their parents/families to drop in to meet teacher, tour classroom, share information and learn about classroom schedules and information.	• Phone calls to parents • Emails to parents • Post invitation notice on school board near where class lists are posted. • Set-up parent table in classroom with student background survey, parent volunteer interest sheet, parent conference sign-up sheet, and Welcome letter with invitation to Back to School Night	• Teacher with help from bilingual parent liaison	• Complete phone calls by 3rd week in August • Host open classroom Sept. 3rd a.m. and Sept. 4th p.m.

example of how a new teacher might chart a plan to translate the vision they created in chapter 1 into an action plan for the coming year.

QUESTIONS

1. What ways can I connect with my students' families and communities before the school year begins?
2. What are my strengths in working with families of ELL and how might I continue to build upon my strengths?
3. Besides sending notes or calling home, how can I regularly reach out to each family in each student's education?

4. How might I utilize my parents in communication with each other?

5. How might I find out if there are parent volunteers to support outreach to other parents/families of ELL?

6. What possibilities exist for utilizing bilingual liaisons to support my work with students and their families?

7. What are some ways in which I might create/strengthen connections with parents/families of my ELL students?

REFERENCES

Allen-Jones, G. L. (2001). *Home-school communications and the use of newsletters.* University Park, IL: Governors State University.

American Association of University Women. (2006). Community programs. Retrieved on September 20, 2006, from http://www.aauw.org/community_programs/index.cfm

Barbre, J., & Hiatt-Michael, D. B. (2004, April). *Parent involvement with home activities that increase preschoolers' first and second language acquisition.* Paper presented at the Educational Research Association Annual Meeting, San Diego, CA.

Bell, S. S. (1996). Kindergartners respond to teacher visits. *Teaching and Change, 4*(1), 50–61.

Bermudez, A. B., & Padron, Y. N. (1998). University-school collaboration that increases minority parents involvement. *Educational Horizons, 66,* 83–86.

Bhavagri, N., & Krolikowski, S. (2000, Spring). *Home-school community visits during an era of reform.* Early Childhood Research and Practice 1. (ERIC Document Reproduction Service No.ED 439851)

Bittle, R. G. (1975). Improving parent–teacher communication through recorded telephone messages. *The Journal of Educational Research, 69*(3), 87–95.

Chavkin, N. F. (1993). Families and schools in a pluralistic society. Albany: State University of New York Press.

Cottle, W. E. (1991). *Improving communications between parents and teachers of middle school age students by the use of the telephone and other techniques.* Ft. Lauderdale, FL: Nova University.

Davies, D., Burch, P., & Johnson, V. (1992, February). A portrait of schools reaching out. *Center on Families, Communities, Schools and Children's Learning. Report No. 1.*

Decker, J., & Majerczyk, D. (2000). *Increasing parent involvement through effective home/school communication.* Unpublished manuscript, Saint Xavier University at Chicago.

Decker, L. Gregg, G., & Decker, V. (1996). *Teachers' manual for parent and community involvement.* Alexanderia, VA: National Community Education Association.

Dodd, E. L., & Lilly, D. H. (1997). Family portfolios: Portraits of children and families. *Preventing School Failure, 4*(2), 57–63.

Education World. (2003, August 19). *Schools find many ways to say welcome back.* Retrieved March, from http://www.educationworld.com/a_admin/admin/admin 319.shtml

EMT Associates Inc. (2005). *Evaluation on the effectiveness of our home visit model and training.* Retrieved March 8, 2006, from http://www.pthvp.org/data.html

Espinosa, L. (1995). *Hispanic parent involvement in early childhood programs.* ERIC Digest, University of Illinois, Urbana.

Foster, S. M. (1994). Successful parent meetings. *Young Children, 60*(1), 78–80.

FUSD Master Plan for English Learners. (2006). Retrieved September 18, 2006, from http://multilingual.fresno.k12.ca.us/mastplan/el9fold/el9.htm

Funkhouser, J. E., & Gonzales, M. R. (1998). *Family involvement in children's education: Successful local approaches.* Washington, DC: Office of Educational Research and Improvement.

Furger, R. (2005). Making connections between home and school. The George Lucas Educational Foundation. Retrieved, from http://www.edutopia.org/php/article. php? id=art_1006

Hiatt-Michael, D. B. (2001). *Home-school communication. Promising practices for family involvement in schools.* Charlotte, NC: Information Age Publishing.

Hiatt-Michael, D. B. (Ed.). (2003). *Promising practices to connect school with the community.* Charlotte, NC: Information Age Publishing.

Hiatt-Michael, D. B. (2006). *Promising practices for parent involvement across the continents.* Charlotte, NC: Information Age Publishing.

Houston Independent School District. (1997). *Absent student assistance program, precinct 7, 1996–97.* Houston, TX: Department of Research and Accountability.

Hunt, C. (2002). *Guess who's coming to dinner: The impact of home visits on English language learners in a multicultural high school.* Retrieved March 2006, from http://gse.gmu.edu/research/lmtip/arp/vol3.htm

Johnstone, T. R., & Hiatt, D. B. (1997, March). *Development of a school-based parent center for low-income new immigrants.* Symposium conducted at the American Educational Research Association Annual Meeting, Chicago, IL.

Kelty, J. (1997). *An examination of Hispanic parent involvement in early childhood programs.* Master's Thesis, Grand Valley State University, MI. (ERIC Document Reproduction Service No. ED420406)

Kyle, D. W., McIntyre, E., Miller, K. B., & Moore, G. H. (2002). *Reaching out: A K–8 resource for connecting families and schools.* Thousand Oaks, CA: Corwin Press.

McCaleb, S. P. (1997). *Building communities of learners.* Mahwah, NJ: Lawrence Erlbaum Associates.

Moles, O. (Ed.). (1999). *Reaching all families: Creating family-friendly schools* [Brochure]. Washington, DC: U.S. Department of Education: Office of Education.

Moles, O. (Ed.). (2000). *Reaching all families: Beginning of the school year activities* [Brochure]. Washington, DC: U.S. Department of Education, Office of Education.

Moll, L. C., & Arnot-Hopffer. (2005). Sociocultural competence in teacher education. *Journal of Teacher Education, 56*(3), 242–247.

Pena, D. (1998, April). *Mexican American parental involvement in site-based management.* Paper presented at the Annual Meeting of the American Educational Research Association. San Diego, CA. (ERIC Document Retrieval Service No. ED 423086)

Pena, D. C. (2000, April). *The social dynamics of parental involvement: Social capital, power, and control.* Paper presented at the American Educational Research Association Annual Meeting, New Orleans, LA.

PICO National Network Case Study. (n.d.). *Parent–teacher home visit project.* Retrieved April 3, 2006, from http://www.piconetwork.org/casestudies/parent-teacher-home-visit-project.pdf

Purrington, L. (1998). El Morro Elementary School Welcome Parents. Laguna Beach Unified School District, CA.

Purrington, L. (2006). *Survey of principals in Southern California.* Unpublished raw data. Pepperdine University, Los Angeles, CA.

Sturrock, C. (2006, January 23). *Teachers go the extra mile at Sankofa Academy, concern for students is a driving force.* San Francisco Chronicle. Retrieved March 3, 2006, from http://www.sfgate.com/cgi-bin/article.cgi?f=/c/a/2006/01/23/bag35griht1.dtl

Taveras, G. (1998). *Home visits from the teachers' perspective.* (ERIC Document Reproduction Service No. ED426775)

U.S. Department of Education. (2002a). *No Child Left Behind act.* Retrieved September 18, 2006, from http://www.ed.gov/legislation/esea02

U.S. Department of Education. (2002b). *Sec.1118. Parental involvement.* Retrieved September 12, 2006, from http://www.ed.gov/legislation/esea/sec1118.html

Winter, M. (1995). *Home visiting: Forging the home-school connection.* U. S. Department of Education. (ERIC Document Retrieval Service No. ED405075)

CHAPTER 5

MAKING YOUR CLASSROOM PARENT-FRIENDLY TO FAMILIES OF ENGLISH LANGUAGE LEARNERS

Hsiu-Zu Ho, Kathy R. Fox, and Margarita Gonzalez

Like we parents don't trust the teachers. We should leave them alone to do their work. We show respect by staying out of the classroom. Besides we don't have any training to be in the classroom.

A parent's role in today's school setting has changed in recent decades from that of only being a school supporter to additionally being an active partner in the education of their child (Berger, 1991; Epstein, 1985; Henderson, 2007; Paratore, Melzi, & Kroll-Sinclair, 1999). Instead of parents being involved only in school fund-raising and special school events, parents also serve as classroom volunteers, designers of home-school communication, and leaders, advocates and decision-makers. The cultural beliefs held by many immigrant families regarding parent involvement typically do not include classroom participation or other types of school involvement. The above quote is an initial response from one immigrant parent on being parent volunteers in the classroom. Many immigrant parents view hands-on involvement in the classroom as inappropriate and disrespectful to the teacher authority (Suarez-Orozco & Suarez-Orozco, 2002). However, visible

Promising Practices for Teachers to Engage Families of English Language Learners, pages 61–85
Copyright © 2007 by Information Age Publishing
All rights of reproduction in any form reserved.

parent engagement in the school is now seen by the educational community as an important part of every child's success (Gonzalez & Chrispeels, n.d.; Hoover-Dempsey & Sandler, 2005). Although immigrant families are typically involved in school-related activities at home (Boethel, 2003), they often are not aware of the school's expectations of them as active partners in their children's education via classroom (as parent assistants) and school activities (e.g., PTA, Open House, fundraisers). Full involvement of English language learner (ELL) families requires additional outreach commitment and efforts from teachers and other school personnel (Boethel, 2003; Mattingly, Prislin, McKenzie, Rodriguez, & Kayzar, 2002) as well as a shift in the parents' perspectives regarding their roles in the classroom and school. Research has shown that parent involvement is critical to students' academic success (Henderson & Mapp, 2002). Furthermore, effects of parent involvement on student achievement differs among ethnic groups within the United States (Hong & Ho, 2005; Keith, et al., 1998) as well as among ethnic groups in other countries (Hiatt-Michael, 2005).

Research suggests that the single most important factor for promoting parent involvement is creating a sense of community between parents and instilling a sense of belonging and efficacy (Ames, 1993; Hoover-Dempsey et al., 2005; Nistler & Maiers, 2000). In developing effective home-school partnerships, the classroom is the logical place to begin to build trust and rapport with diverse families. For teachers, as discussed in the preceding chapters, it is important to get to know the parent community, understand their perspectives and expectations, and utilize the cultural and cognitive resources of the home as part of the classroom. Despite the importance of home-school partnerships for children's academic success, aspects of parent involvement are often not covered in teacher education programs and many new teachers do not feel adequately prepared to work with families (Epstein, Sanders, & Clark, 1999; Weiss, Kreider, Lopez, & Chatman, 2005). A variety of strategies are needed in order for teachers to be able to successfully engage families from diverse cultures. This chapter provides practices that teachers can implement in order to make their classroom as well as the school parent-friendly to families of ELL. Teachers indeed play an important role in fostering the home-school partnership by creating an inclusive classroom climate and promoting a sense of belonging to a vital classroom community among the families.

STEPS TO TAKE PRIOR TO THE BEGINNING
OF THE SCHOOL YEAR

The beginning of the school year is a key time to communicate with families. How a teacher presents herself/himself to the students and their families is an important part of the parent–teacher communication. This relationship can begin before the first day of class.

End-of-Year Classroom Preview

At some schools, teachers made their classrooms accessible to incoming parents and students at the end of the year (usually during the last month of the school year). For example, in one local school, a sixth grade class invited the fifth-grade class and parents to an end-of-the year event to share story books that they had written, bound and illustrated. Other artifacts of various classroom projects and activities that were undertaken throughout the year were also available for view. In this event, parents were able to meet the teachers for their children's upcoming year and see the evidence of parent involvement in their classrooms. The incoming parents had opportunities to interact with the teacher as well as parents of the class and learn about the norms, routines, and expectations of the upcoming classrooms.

Welcome Receptions

Other teachers hold a welcoming tea in their classroom or other types of receptions a few days prior to the first day of school in order to meet classroom families. The meeting is useful to explain homework policies, hand out forms necessary for school lunch programs and other beginning of the school year information, and meet other families. In this way, parents and teachers begin to see themselves as a community. Teachers can promote the sense of community by organizing "icebreakers" for parents to get to know one another and share information. One teacher has students introduce their parents and tell something about them. "*This is my mother. She was born in Laos. She makes beautiful Hmong story cloth quilts called "pa'ndau.*" Another teacher uses a Parent Bingo game in which items for the game include: "*Find someone who was born in the same month as yourself,*" or "*Find someone who has the same number of children as you,*" or "*Find someone who changed careers when they immigrated to the United States.*"

Welcome Signs

Immigrant families often step into "unknown territory" when they go to their children's school. Bilingual visual aids will send the message right from the start that the school welcomes all families to be partners in the

TABLE 5.1
Welcome in Other Languages

English	Welcome to our classroom!
Spanish	Bienvenidos a nuestro salon de clase!
Mandarin Chinese	Huanying laidao women de jiaoshi!
Tagalog (Philippines)	Maligayang pagdating sa ating silid-aralan
Hindi (India)	Humare kaakshaala mein aapka swagat hai!
Vietnamese	Han hoan chao mung quy quan khach da den tham quan truong hoc cua chung toi!
French	Bienvenus a notre classe!
Korean	Juhui kyushilul bangmoon hajushulse kamsahamita!

education of their children. Display a welcome sign on classroom doors or inside the classroom written in the languages of ELL families. Table 5.1 provides English Romanization of "Welcome to our classroom" in some of the most common languages of ELL families in the United States.[1]

Open Classrooms During Preparation Days

Simple steps that a classroom teacher can take, such as leaving the classroom door open during those last preparation days (before school begins) send a message to families that they are welcome to come in and visit the classroom, meet the teacher and get a sense of the classroom environment. Most schools post class lists on a school communication board a few days before the year begins. When parents and children visit the school to read the lists they often walk around the school to find the classroom as well. A teacher can simply post a note on the class list inviting parents to stop by the classroom. A teacher who is prepared for this opportunity can use this initial meeting as a time to set the tone for future communications. It may even be possible to "enlist" parents as classroom volunteers at this time. This may be especially helpful for minority language parents who might be less likely to raise questions in a larger parent meeting.

One elementary school teacher shared that one of the most successful strategies in making the classroom family friendly included inviting parents as well as the students to help during the preparation days. Parents conducted tasks with their children, such as labeling folders and notebooks, sharpening pencils, and cutting paper and in doing so families felt an important part of the classroom community right from the beginning, a sense of belonging to the school (J. Scalzo, personal communication, 2006). This opportunity for the classroom teacher and families to meet and interact initiated an important home-school partnership.

As discussed in detail in Chapter 3, home visits by teachers are ideal. Visiting a child and parent in their home not only enables the teacher to understand first-hand the cultural background of the family but helps to reduce the stress and anxiety that both the child and parent may feel on the first day of school. For the very young children, it may help to alleviate the separation anxiety that is frequently evident with preschool or kindergarten students (V. Herrity, personal communication, 2006).

Contacting Parents via Telephone or Letter

Telephone calls are another way to meet parents before the school year begins. Setting the goal of phoning five parents a day during the week prior to school opening is a realistic goal for teachers. Keeping the conversation brief but flexible is sufficient for setting a courteous and respectful tone that shows interest in the child and family. To assist a teacher who is unfamiliar with the language of the family, a script can be prepared and practiced for communicating basic information over the telephone (Hunt, 2002). This effort demonstrates to the family that the teacher acknowledges their home language and that he or she is willing to share in language learning for the purpose of communication. A parent letter may also be sent prior to the first day of school. This letter should be translated into the home languages of the children. Checking cumulative files or registration documentation or asking the child's prior teachers are important ways to identify the home language. The letter should include up-to-date information, such as how many students are in the classroom and news of school events for the first day and/or week. The tone of the letter should be professional but friendly, adult to adult, rather than from an authoritarian tone. The teacher's letter may describe an open-door policy, provide personal information, and outline opportunities when parents can drop by. Many teachers use this letter to ask parents about their children as well. The letter invites parents to share their perceptions of their child (strengths and challenges) and share their expectation goals for the student during the coming year. The letter also invites the parent to come to the classroom and share family traditions and customs and aspects of their native country (see section below on "Incorporating Family Cultures in the Classroom Curriculum"). By communicating in this manner, the teacher sends the message that all families are valued.

Another point to consider is the type of contact information to provide. Teachers can find out what language parents would prefer for future correspondence and if email, phone or mail is preferred. To demonstrate respect for their family time, teachers may ask parents to give the best times and numbers to call them. In return, provide parents with similar information regarding times to contact the teacher. This may include a schedule of after class hours, an email address or the teacher's home number with appropriate hours to call. The point is that to have true communication it must be bidirectional. One of the coauthors of this chapter recalls a parent's remark: "*My child's teacher often calls us during dinner time to report his behavior in class. She even once called me at work. But when I asked her how I could contact her, she told me she was not able to give me that information.*" Finally, ending the letter on a positive note is important; in particular the letter ends with an invitation: "*I hope to see you very soon in our classroom,*" sending the message again that all parents are welcome.

An attached page may be provided by the teacher that has specific questions regarding the child's strengths and challenges, parents' goals and expectations for the year, concerns the parents may have, and any special traditions that the parents may want to share. The page also inquires about the preferred ways of contact (email or phone), time and contact information.

It is important to translate the letter into the languages of classroom families. If a teacher is unable to translate the letter and/or other materials, another teacher, an instructional assistant, the school secretary, a bilingual parent, or even a student who is competent in both languages may be able to assist. Many school districts have paid translators as well, although this generally requires advance notice. Even if the letter is not translated word for word, a version of the letter in the home language with the original in English copied on the back sends a message of cultural inclusiveness and respect.

AS THE SCHOOL YEAR BEGINS

Meet and Greet

The practice of meeting and greeting all students and parents the first day of school conveys a message that the school values their presence in the learning environment. A powerful tool to initiate a sense of community is to learn greetings in the parents' primary languages. An elementary school in the Los Angeles area implemented this practice on a daily basis with successful results. The practice of greeting and shaking each student's and parent's hands by the teachers as well as the principal began as a way to demonstrate that the school welcomes and cares about their students and families. Soon it became institutionalized on campus by all staff, children and families. The three major ethnic groups (White, Latino, and African American) who typically had not previously interacted with each other, began to feel appreciated and respected. This daily practice initiated a social network that created a positive climate and atmosphere in the school (Gonzalez & Rivero, 2006). One of the coauthors of this chapter recalls the first day her older son entered kindergarten and his teacher came up and greeted her son by name as he entered the front of the school. The mother was surprised that the teacher knew who her son was and will never forget the warm welcome of the teacher on that important first day of school for her and her son. It was an important first step that positively impacted the remainder of the elementary school years.

The first day of school is also an important opportunity to demonstrate to parents that a teacher values their involvement in the classroom. The practice of welcoming parents and their child into the classroom by name and having extra adult-sized chairs available for the parents sends the message to parents that their presence is anticipated. Take the time to shake hands and spend some time with the parents on this day. It shows that you value their presence and knowledge of their child's family.

Visiting the Classroom

An effective way to help parents be partners of students' learning and develop a bridge between the home and school is to promote classroom visits for parent observations of their children's daily school activities. A visit of their children's classrooms can be a successful learning experience for families of ELL. These families bring their own learning experiences from their home countries and need to personally experience and see through their own eyes what their children are learning in their new country to be able to assist them. A good strategy for bringing parents into the classroom is to involve the students in the organization of their parents' visits. Civil and Quintos (2006) tell the successful story of an immigrant mother whose daughter encouraged her to visit her classroom, "Come to learn how they teach here, come see that I am all right." The Verizon Options Initiative at Isla Vista Elementary School in Goleta, California, incorporates parent visitations of their child's classroom as an integral part of their family literacy program. It enables the parent to develop a better understanding of the educational system prior to becoming a regular assistant in the classroom, observing the educational process in which their child is engaged (Herrity, Ho, Dixon, & Brown, 2006). This not only makes the parent feel more comfortable in the classroom but also provides a clearer understanding of how the parent can reinforce concepts that have been learned at school when the child does his/her homework at home. After a series of classroom observations, the parent begins to take on additional volunteer responsibilities in the classroom such as reading stories to a group of children or providing individualized support to children.

Classroom visits are better organized if they are accompanied by brief pre- and post-visit meetings. For example, during the pre-visit, parents can be informed about the observation norms and receive prompts to guide their observation, such as: what do you see that the students are learning, how is the instruction driven (e.g., textbook, hands-on), how is your child responding? At the end of the visit, the teacher can learn about the parents' observations and discuss strategies to support their child's learning at home. In order to minimize interruption of classroom instruction, teachers can schedule the parents' visits accordingly.

Parent Job List

One way to ensure that parents feel welcomed and included from the beginning of the school year is to introduce parent involvement opportunities on the first day. In order for this to be successful, however, teachers and parents must come to a consensus on what involvement looks like in the classroom and understand the expectations that each other hold. A preschool teacher once reported that the parents in her program were generally new to schooling in the United States. When parents were required to do eight hours of involvement or volunteer in the classroom each month in order for their children to attend, some were confused: "What could they do in a classroom? They were not trained teachers." In response, on the first day of school, the preschool teacher made available a Parent Jobs List to enable parents to sign up for specific jobs she needed done in the classroom. The list included brief details of each job, the days needed and the approximate time required to complete the task. With this simple job, list parents could see that parent involvement included a variety of tasks, and that each of these tasks was necessary to make the classroom run smoothly. While the tasks vary by teachers as well as by grade level, a few examples for the elementary grade levels on the list are: copy and collate class-work, correct weekly spelling/vocabulary tests, prepare materials for the weekly folder, distribute materials in students' cubbies, and wash paint cups and brushes. It is important that the list is translated into the languages of all the families in the classroom.

The practice of having a small white board as a message center is an easy way to list day-to-day tasks for parents. Messages such as, "Sort math materials into cups for tomorrow's lesson" (with a sample along side the materials), are quick and nonthreatening ways to involve parents in the classroom. In addition to a job list, this parent message board located in the Parent Work Space (discussed below) is also a good place to include resource information that is provided by teachers as well as fellow parents.

Another way to organize parent involvement in the classroom is to have parent volunteers sign up for different times of the day (e.g., M 8:30–10:30; 10:30–12:30) and complete specific tasks that the teacher has listed for the day. Parent involvement can include a variety of tasks and these tasks should be organized for parents to get optimum understanding and participation. The job list gives parents ideas for helping in ways that they may not have previously viewed as a classroom job, especially for parents who did not attend schools in the United States. While parent job lists are more frequently seen in preschool through elementary grade levels, they can also be useful in the middle and high-school levels. More frequently, in middle and high-school levels, teachers are looking for parents to share their special talents and professional experience rather than engage in tasks that help to run the classroom more smoothly.

Incorporating Family Cultures in the Classroom Curriculum

In addition to helping the teacher run the classroom smoothly, ELL parents can be an important academic/learning resource for the classroom. Parents can contribute to the classroom curriculum by sharing their talents as well as aspects of the home cultures. By incorporating the "lived experiences" of students—the common cultural activities of the home as part of the curriculum, the invaluable strengths of diversity can be realized (Gonzalez & Moll, 2002; Moll, Amanti, Neff, & Gonzalez, 1992). In one school, a teacher invites parents on a rotational basis to the classroom on Fridays during their typical social studies class to share aspects of classroom families' culture and home country (e.g., history, geography, literature, architecture, religion, food, dance, and music). Through these types of presentations, students are taught topics that range from the history/geography and politics of Korea; the architecture of Chinese temples; the mathematical engineering behind the Mayan pyramids; the music of and steps to Spanish folkloric dances; the celebration of India's Festival of Lights—the Diwali; the pictograph-based written language of China; themes of Filipino folk stories; and how to make Vietnamese spring rolls, Mexican tamales, or Tandoori dishes. Some teachers invite parents on a regular basis to come into the classroom and share aspects of their profession with the students. Students may gain knowledge about the training of a tai-chi instructor, the operations of a restaurant business or a grocery store, the mathematics that are employed in the lives of a seamstress, architect, carpenter or building contractor or the science that is utilized in the lives of a farmer, mechanic, or engineer.

Another way of incorporating family cultures into the classroom curriculum is to engage students as oral historians by interviewing others, such as family and community members, when drawing on lived experience as a resource (Yeager & Elder, 2005). For example, one student presented to his class a powerful interview of his stepfather who was a Vietnam veteran. Another student presented a moving interview of his grandmother who was a Japanese internee during World War II (E. Yeager, personal communication, 2006). In another classroom, students interviewed their parents about their (students') name—how their parents decided on their first and middle (if applicable) names as well as any historical information they may have about their last name (J. Scalzo, personal communication, 2006). The students conduct the interview and take notes. The story of their name is placed with their picture and displayed in a timely fashion so that parents can see the display during their Back to School event.

In some classrooms, parents support in learning activities such as "Reading Centers," or "Math Activities/Games"; others conduct presentations during Social Studies or Art/Music/Dance. One ELL parent who was a regular volunteer in his daughter's preschool worked "was terrific at building blocks with the children in the blocks area and also loved doing puzzles with them. Having these kinds of both verbal and nonverbal action-oriented activities on the job list encourages parents to participate in helping students learn even when speaking different languages" (E. Yeager, personal communication, 2006).

Cross-Cultural Differences in Teacher Expectation

Teachers also have cross-cultural differences in their perceptions of activities that students and parents should engage in at school. During an exchange where teachers from Taiwan and the U.S. visited each other's respective schools, "puzzling" aspects revealed by each nation's team included expectations of students' involvement in school fundraisers and custodial-type services. The Taiwanese teachers were puzzled by the expectation of student and family involvement in school fundraisers such as "jogathons" in the U.S. schools. *"Why do you have children involved in raising money for your school?"* Likewise, American teachers were taken aback by the custodial-type services required of the students in Taiwan. *"Why do you have students mopping the floors and cleaning the boards and windows in your classrooms?"* While one culture instilled in young students pride and ownership through family involvement in contributing to the school by raising funds, another culture instilled pride and ownership by helping to keep one's school tidy and clean. Just like teachers, parents from various cultural backgrounds have different expectations of classroom activities and engagement.

Family Display in Classroom

Visual displays of students' home cultures on classroom boards and walls send a message of caring, respect and inclusiveness to students and their families. For example, students may make "My Family" collages that incorporate photos of family members and pets, drawings and text depicting foods, traditions and holidays of their home cultures. A written narrative may accompany each collage. A "Map of our Families Origins" depicting where students and their families were born may also be displayed. Students may mark these locations on the map with pins, the countries flag, and each student and their families' name. Charts on classroom walls can display languages spoken by the students, languages spoken by their parents and particular phrases regarding rights, respect and responsibility written in the various languages represented.

Many classrooms feature a particular student as the Student of the Week, going through the class roster as the year progresses. A display board may include the child's family and cultural background. A week prior to the student's turn for the honor, a Student of the Week form is sent home. The open-ended form include questions such as: "Where was (*child's name*) born?" "How do you celebrate (*child's name*) birthday?" What are (*child's name*) hobbies? "What is (*child's name*) favorite food?" The family may be invited to send photographs that the child can help label and mount on the Student of the Week display board along with the Student of the Week questionnaire. A favorite activity, game, talent, or collection of objects can be shared on Friday of the student's special week, giving the child another opportunity to share cultural artifacts relevant to his or her home.

AS THE SCHOOL YEAR PROGRESSES

Parent Work Space

As the school year progresses, it is important to continue to engage parents. A parent volunteer bulletin board may be placed in the school office that welcomes parents, provides a space for them to sign in and pick up a volunteer name badge which recognizes them as a volunteer in the school. Now that the Job List has been set up and parents begin to come in, it is important that the parents know where to be in the classroom. Just as in your home, as a matter of courtesy you would invite parents to sit down and be comfortable, the same is implied in the classroom. A designated parent table can make parents feel that their presence is expected and valued. The Parent Work Space demonstrates a tone of professionalism given to the parent's role. The space also provides a designated area for the children to focus on the activities they might do with the parent. A clearly-labeled Parent Work Box can be made available in the parent work space. In this box there should be adult-sized scissors, markers used for lettering and others for grading. A list of specific activities provided by the teacher (for that day or week or an "If you have extra time . . . " list) will enable parents to feel that their volunteer time is well spent. Seeing their parent participate and making contributions to the classroom community also gives the child a sense of pride.

As the teacher gets to know her/his class and which children can benefit from one-on-one time with an adult, she/he may develop a list of children for parents to read with, along with suggested titles in the Parent Work Box. Providing stickers and/or award sheets in the box for parents to give to children adds closure to the activity. If a specific academic area needs to be addressed, such as subtraction facts or putting words in alphabetical order, a packet may be included in the box with the child's name noted: "*Please ask Sonia to play Subtraction Bingo with you. You can include two other children of her choice as well. Instructions for the game are in the lid of the box.*" Making sure that the activities in the box are ones the child is comfortable and/or familiar with ensures success with the learning experience.

Classroom Newsletter

A classroom newsletter (see also Chapter 4) created with input from the children, for example, can be issued on a regular basis. These newsletters can be reproduced in a consistent color and sent home on the same day of every week (every two weeks or every month), making them easily recognizable to both children and parents. The practice of having student artwork and/or writing included in the newsletter provides interest and reflects a child-centered philosophy. The practice of putting personal notes in the classroom newsletter, such as recognizing parent volunteers or thanking parents for helping out with specific projects, creates a sense of community as well as encourages continued involvement.

Another important step for the classroom teacher to take is to read the newsletter to the class at the end of the day before it is distributed. In many homes of second language learners, the child is the language broker, or translator for the parents. By reading through the letter with the class, the child has a better understanding and will be able to explain things beyond the words on the page. For young readers putting icons or picture cues on the page, such as a star by where the parents fill in information, will help the child to remember that this cued part of the letter must be returned. Reading the newsletter with the class before leaving at the end of the day, pointing out key parts of the letter by cued symbols, and highlighting vocabulary will assist the child. The important part of the message here is that the child and parents have access to the letter, by either translation, picture cues, or both.

Telephone Communication

A teacher who goes the extra step to make personal phone calls to the parents telling of their child's progress rather than in terms of problems or negative situations is setting a tone of respect and pride for her/his students. Such calls counteract the feeling of many parents that schools only contact them when there is bad news. The practice of making two positive phone calls a week (a realistic goal) can help the teacher manage this system of parent communication. Teachers can give parents brief ideas for home learning activities that reflect a similar classroom activity on an "as-needed" basis by phone. An outgrowth of personalized telephone communication at some schools is the parent call-in where teachers set up a regular call-in hour on a weekly or biweekly basis. During this time, parents can call to discuss their questions or concerns.

Parent–Teacher Conferences

Regular conferences for all families are an essential building block of home-school communication. Conferences provide a time and space for listening and sharing and establishing partnerships. During this time parents provide important perspectives and information that can be extremely valuable. Teachers often receive little training for the vital task of the parent conference and many use them to explain the criteria and grades used on report cards and schedule them right after a reporting period. A successful event applied in many schools, particularly at upper elementary, middle and high school grade levels, is the student-led parent conference, in which students prepare a portfolio with their work and attend the conference with their family. This type of conference is different from the traditional teacher–parent conference by giving more responsibility to the students and promoting student self-assessment and parent involvement. Each student leads their personal conference with his/her family, sharing their new learning and progress as well as interests and goals while the teacher walks around each family to exchange conversations and discussions about how to help the student move to the next cognitive level. The benefits of these conferences for students, parents and teachers have been shown in past research studies. For example, Austin (1994) reported that as students reflected on their own learning, sought the views of others, and prepared their own portfolios, they came to know themselves as learners. A number of studies (e.g., Bailey & Guskey, 2001; Hackman, 1997; Syverson, 2006) provide evidence of the success of student-led conferences in many schools throughout the nation. These types of conferences appear to be more successful when teachers create a climate that empowers the student and promotes collaboration with diverse families.

Below we provide a list of activities that teachers can do before, during and after the conferences to successfully meet and establish long-term relationships and partnerships with families of ELL:

Before the Conference

- Survey parents to identify their needs, concerns and time preferences.
- Ask bilingual parents to volunteer as translators and let parents know that translators are available.
- Call parents (or ask bilingual parent volunteers to call) in advance to arrange their conference time and tell them how important it is for the child.
- Schedule flexible times to provide options for working parents and those with more than one child in the school.
- Use various means of communication to invite families (personal invitations when students are dropped off or picked-up, invitation letters from the students, newsletters, posters at your door).
- Help students prepare their portfolios with samples of work and reflections on their learning.
- Create a comfortable and private physical environment providing enough adult-sized chairs and with no desk separating teacher from parent.

During the Conference

- Establish rapport by asking parents about their work or a personal interest/hobby they have.
- Use a positive approach to emphasize the child's strengths and unique qualities.
- Ask parents to share their view of the child's strengths and interests.
- Establish priorities for the child and select one or two areas for growth and improvement that the parents and child can work on until the next conference. Do not overwhelm them.
- Listen and learn from the parents. Ask them to share their concerns, ideas and questions and involve them in creating solutions to problems. While you listen, take notes from what they say.

- Provide resources and materials that parents may check out to use at home to support their child's learning.
- Do not assume that families know the school system or what you expect from them. Together, brainstorm ideas for how you can work as partners to help the child succeed at school.
- Arrange dates for your next conference and the best times for you to call or visit the families.

After the Conference

- Keep a journal about the conference and have a note for each family; write their concerns, questions and suggestions and take next steps to follow through.
- Keep parents informed of any steps that you or other school staff have taken and follow up on actions or concerns parents expressed.
- Follow-up with a phone call or a note to show your appreciation and commitment for working with the family as a partner.

Special Parent Days

As the school year progresses parent involvement may include special parent events, when parents and/or family members are invited into the classroom for special activities. The most common types of these events are classroom parties or holiday programs. With parent involvement, classrooms may celebrate traditional ethnic holidays that are meaningful to their families (e.g., Cinco de Mayo, the Lunar New Year, Diwali, Dia de los Muertos, Kwanza, Lantern Festival, Mid-autumn Festival, Boxing Day). In some schools special parent days are regularly scheduled for additional parent involvement purposes, such as parent education, parent involvement in a project and/or family literacy. To inform parents about new report cards being distributed that included standards rather than letter grades, teachers in one school combined classes so that other teachers could lead parent meetings in different languages to explain the forms.

In another school, one event that brought more parents in the classroom—particular mothers in this event—was a grade level project in which parents participated in one of three "Sew in Days." Sewing machines were set up in the back of one classroom to make simple book bags for the children in all four kindergarten classrooms of that school. Parents and teachers loaned their sewing machines for the three days and other parents donated fabric. Eighty book bags were made as a result of this 3-day event. More important, the parents became more familiar with various aspects of their child's school, their daily classroom activities and had more opportunities to interact with the school staff. This event helped to increase the parents' sense of belonging to the classroom community and the school. It promoted social networking between parents and teachers of diverse backgrounds. The "noise" of the project was a productive one. Children were able to see the presence and involvement of their parents in their school as well as observe the process of making the bags from start to finish. The children took pride in the bags the parents made and carried them throughout the year.

To support children's literacy growth, in one project, parent participants attended school with their children one Friday of each month (Nistler & Maiers, 2000). They participated in poetry activities that could be practiced in the home, in cooking lessons that validated how food preparation activities in the home could incorporate literacy, as well as in music and science activities, and math and literacy stations. In addition to the scheduled activities, the teacher met with individual parents during this time. Parents were encouraged to write in journals about their experiences.

Often events involving food provide a more relaxed and informal setting where parents feel comfortable in giving feedback, including ideas for volunteer activities as well as how to become more involved. An after school parent meeting with snacks prepared by the students and invitations made by the students will encourage parent attendance with their children's involvement as a motivator. Some teachers invite parents to come to school on a selected day for an informal potluck breakfast (organized by parent volunteers) to give parents an opportunity to meet with the teacher and with each other. These events can be held in a selected classroom with teachers partnering to release each other for a brief time to converse with parents or during the regular classroom morning schedule, with a small group of parents invited on a rotational basis. The parents are encouraged to stay and observe the morning routine.

Field Trips

Class field trips are also a good way to involve parents in their child's schooling. Teachers can use the extra supervision; parents have an opportunity to be involved in the educational event; and the trips increase parent–teacher communication and interaction. Parent volunteers are often requested for field trips taken during the school day and this often limits participation of working parents; although given enough notice, some parents may take time off from work to participate. One teacher who taught fourth grade in the Hawaiian island of Molokai, where most of his ELL families were Filipino, remarked on a successful weekend field trip that he reflected as having been instrumental to building a strong sense of community.

My students and I organized two excursions to a site where we were working on a native reforestation project. Parents and whole families were invited to both field trips, one which occurred earlier in the year, on a weekday, and the second, which took place on a Saturday. While both events enjoyed strong parent participation, the Saturday trip attracted an enormous amount of extended family participation, including student siblings, grandparents, and cousins. I attributed the increased participation to the greater availability of parents on a Saturday and to the "word of mouth" that had spread about the relaxed, nonthreatening, and fun nature of the first trip. The children actually helped draw their parents into participating in the Saturday trip, based on the success of the first trip. These field trips were truly family affairs where we shared lunch, potluck style, and became familiar with each other over the course of learning about the stated focus of our trip—the cultural and ecological significance of the area we were reforesting with native plants. I remember thinking, in the moment, about how valuable this event would be to building a community of support for this class. As it turned out, it helped provide a foundation for an extremely successful school year marked by strong parental support. Participation that year was marked by the noticeable increased involvement of ELL parents who previously had not been as active in their children's classroom activities. (J. Moniz, personal communication, 2006)

Open House During the School Year

Schools need to share information about their programs with all parents. One widespread approach is the open house which is a great way to welcome families to the school. See Chapter 4 for discussion on open houses prior to the beginning of school. Signs/banners that welcome the families in their own languages reflect recognition of and respect for the ELL families in the school. See Table 5.2 for some of the most common languages of ELL families in the United States.

The open house works best if schools hold them just a few times a year and schedule them at times of low calendar conflict. Open houses are successful when they meet the real needs of parents. The best way to insure success is to involve parents in the planning and get their ideas. A good way to get suggestions for the next open house is to get feedback during the previous open house by having a box for comments and feedback. Moles (1996) suggests considering three P's (planning, publicity and preparation) when organizing open houses. The following is an adaptation of Moles' list of suggestions for the organization of open houses that is particularly sensitive to families of ELL.

TABLE 5.2
Welcome Banner Translations

English	Welcome, thank you for coming to our school!
Spanish	Bienvenidos, gracias por venir a nuestra escuela!
Mandarin Chinese	Huanying, xiexie nimen laidao women xuexiao!
Tagalog	Mabuhay, maraming salamat sa pag-dating ninyo sa ating eskuwelahan!
Hindi	Aapka swagat karte hein, humari paatshaala mein aane ka dhanyawad!
Vietnamese	Han hoan chao mung quy quan khach da den tham quan truong hoc cua chung toi!
French	Bienvenus, merci d'etre venus nous rejoinder a notre ecole!
Korean	Annyeonghaseyo. bangmoon haejushulse kamsahamita!

Planning and Preparation

Schedule the open house about a month after classes start so that teachers are familiar with their students and have enough time to establish contacts with families and parent volunteers. A district-wide open house should be carefully planned with neighbor schools, so that each school holds the event on different evenings. This will facilitate the attendance of families that have children in more than one school and teachers who have school-age children in other schools. Teachers should set high expectations among all students for their families to attend and make sure to have enough bilingual staff or parent volunteers that speak the families' languages. Teachers can help students organize the classroom presentation before the day of the Open House event so that children can practice presenting their work to their parents. Ask the children to select two or three activities/projects they want their parents to see before the teacher presentation begins. This will help to provide a "preview" of the teacher's information.

Publicity

The whole school staff should carefully plan a publicity campaign for the open house in the school and community. A local school had a great parent attendance rate when the students designed personal invitations for their parents in their home language. These invitations were mailed from the school explaining in detail the event and the transportation and childcare that the school would provide. Teachers can work with students on an art project to prepare posters and flyers for the open house using graphics that represent what parents will find in the event. These posters can be hung in visible places in the community such as local grocery stores, businesses and the public library. Additionally, parent volunteers that speak the families' languages may call all parents, particularly new parents, a day or so before the event to personally invite them. On the day of the event, use the loud speaker to remind all children and parents that the school staff is eager to meet their parents that evening at the open house.

Welcoming Environment

Families of ELL need to find a warm and inviting atmosphere in the school. The appearance of the school building and facilities contribute to create a family-friendly open house. The school staff may prepare a road map with clear signs and pathways with numbers that direct parents to the various facilities. Bilingual support staff may be available to guide families around the building. The school's annual report, handbooks, information packets or other items of interest to parents in various languages. The school bulletin board should be updated with news and important information for families. Teachers can prepare an art project with their students that reflects the diversity of their families (e.g., flags, pictures, maps). A welcoming event that was successfully implemented in one high school included the school's band and chorus, who played and sang folkloric music around the school before and after the open house activities.

Open House Program

Teacher and staff presentations should be both informative and enjoyable. The open house usually starts with a welcoming session, led by the principal, in which he or she introduces the staff and the school's philosophy. Next may be a guided tour of the facilities, led by support teachers and parent volunteers that speak the families' languages. Teachers should schedule ample time for parents to meet in their children's classrooms and become familiar with the classroom curriculum and expectations. Parents and teachers can discuss how they would like to partner and families should have the opportunity to ask questions about the upcoming year. Teachers can demonstrate some of the activities that students engaged in during the previous year and prepare some activities that parents can engage in with their children during the open house. Provide opportunities for families to engage one-to-one with their children's teachers. For middle and high school levels, the open house may include a "mock day" where parents go to the various classes/schedules of their child's typical school day (e.g., fifteen minutes per period).

Teacher Presentations

The following are some suggestions for classroom teachers on preparing their classroom presentation:

- Begin your presentation with a brief video segment of the class in action with regard to a particular project;
- Prepare handouts with graphics that reinforce your presentations;
- Prepare an interesting class activity with parents and children; and
- Display unfinished student work to give parents a preview of a project in progress.

Classroom Self Assessment

In looking into ways to make the classroom environment more friendly to families of ELL, teachers and other school personnel may want to conduct a self assessment of the practices in their classrooms and schools. The following "Family-Friendly Classroom Checklist" consists of 36 items that measure three areas: Outreach to Families; School Climate and Culture; and Family Responsiveness. The development of this tool was based on several teacher and parent involvement surveys created by coauthor Margarita Gonzalez. While as a beginning teacher you may not be able to have control of a number of these aspects of the school, you can implement many of them in your own classrooms and suggest others to your administrators.

FAMILY-FRIENDLY CLASSROOM
SELF ASSESSMENT CHECKLIST

Assess whether you have implemented the following practices to make your classroom friendly to ELL families:

1. Outreach to Families.
    - I greet and talk with parents when they drop-off and pick-up their children.
    - I use a personal approach (e.g., face-to-face, personal phone call) to connect with each family.
    - I ask the most involved parents to contact those that are less involved.

- I use translators to communicate with parents that speak languages other than English.
- I assess my families' needs and interests and include them in my classroom activities.
- I include various classroom activities for parents to participate in throughout the year.
- I delegate classroom responsibilities to parents by providing them with a specific job list.
- I schedule special days for parents and other whole-family events throughout the year.
- I schedule events at various times considering the availability and working hours of our diverse families.
- I request or facilitate transportation for parents' meetings and activities.
- I request childcare services for families with younger children for special events.
- I have informational materials available in various formats (e.g., printed, audio, video).

2. Classroom Climate and Culture. *In my classroom:*
   - I welcome families and students from diverse linguistic and socio-cultural backgrounds.
   - I view families as partners to our learning community.
   - I honor the cultures and traditions of my classroom families.
   - I know my students' families.
   - I facilitate informal gatherings for families in the classroom community to get to know one another as well as to meet school personnel.
   - I welcome parents to visit and observe my classroom at any time.
   - I have assigned a place in my classroom for parent volunteers.
   - I acknowledge and build on the life experiences, strengths and talents of my students' families.
   - I incorporate the knowledge, values, traditions and experiences of the home as important resources for the classroom community.
   - I create a safe and trusting atmosphere in my classroom.
   - I provide my students' parents with information, resources and support to guide their child's education.
   - I have parent liaison(s) who help to increase the involvement of parents from diverse backgrounds.

3. Family Responsiveness. *My students' families:*
   - Feel comfortable to talk to me about various aspects of my class.
   - Feel comfortable to talk to me about their child's progress.
   - Participate in the activities organized for classroom parents/families.

- Are aware that aspects of their home culture are recognized and valued in my classroom.
- Volunteer in my classroom.
- Contribute aspects of their family culture to our classroom learning environment.
- Work with the school counselor to develop a plan for their child's academic program.

Classrooms and schools need to be places in which all families are welcomed and are active partners and collaborators in their child's learning. By building a strong sense of community in their classrooms, teachers are instrumental in helping to break down the cultural barriers to meaningful family involvement (Weiss et al., 2005). The teacher–parent partnership needs to truly be bidirectional; that is, it cannot simply be a one-way attempt to transmit classroom values and practices to the home, but need to include sincere and diligent efforts to understand and incorporate the knowledge, values and experiences of the home as important resources for the classroom curriculum. Only through this bidirectional approach can we build "classroom-like homes" and "home like classrooms" where overlapping influences in students' lives interact and share common goals (Epstein, 2001).[2]

An early childhood educator stated that after almost thirty years of teaching, *"I realize that what parents and I can do together benefits the child far more than anything I can do alone"* (Checkley, 2000, p. 4). With increased parental involvement in aspects of the child's schooling, not only is the child positively affected cognitively, socially, and emotionally, but the teacher's classroom and school are enhanced by the resources brought in by the family members. Making parents feel welcomed, providing opportunities for active parental engagement in the classroom, and seeing children watch their parents collaborate as resources to their teacher are examples of powerful "small wins" with powerful implications (Neuman, Caparelli, & Kee, 1988; Nistler & Maiers, 2000).

QUESTIONS TO CONSIDER

1. In what ways can teachers make *all* parents feel welcome and incorporate their talents in the classroom?
2. In what ways can we incorporate the cultural and cognitive resources of the home into our classroom curriculum?
3. Why do some classrooms have a supportive parent community when others are almost nonexistent? In what ways can teachers help to promote and develop that parent community?

4. Why do parents participate in one event but not in another? What are the elements of a successful parent/family school event?

5. What school-wide activities promote parent involvement in the classroom? In what ways can the school help to promote parent involvement?

NOTES

1. As reported by the Center for Immigration Studies, the top ten countries based on the top sending nation from where U.S. immigrants come from are: Mexico, China/Hong Kong/Taiwan, Philippines, India, El Salvador, Vietnam, Cuba, Dominican Republic, Canada, Korea (Camarota, 2005).

2. These terms are modified from Epstein's work that uses "family-like schools" and "school-like families."

REFERENCES

Ames, C. (1993). How school-to-home communications influence parent beliefs and perceptions. *Equity and Choice, 9*(3), 44–49.

Austin, T. (1994). *Changing the view: Student-led parent conferences.* Portsmouth, NH: Heinemann.

Bailey, J. M., & Guskey, T. R. (2001). *Implementing student-led conferences.* Thousand Oaks, CA: Corwin Press.

Berger, E. H. (1991). Parent involvement: Yesterday and today. *The Elementary School Journal, 91*(3), Special Issue: Educational Partnerships: Home-School Community, 209–219.

Boethel, M. (2003). *Diversity: School, family, & community connections* [Annual synthesis]. Austin, TX: Southwest Educational Development Laboratory.

Camarota, S. A., (2005). *Immigrants at mid-Decade: A snapshot of America's foreign-born population in 2005.* Center for Immigration Studies. Retrieved September 25, 2006 from http://www.cis.org/articles/2005/back1405.html

Checkley, K. (2000). Supporting children by supporting families: A family-centered approach to educating young children. *Curriculum Update Newsletter,* 4–8.

Civil, M., & Quintos, B. (2006). *Engaging families in children's mathematical learning: Classroom visits with Latina mothers.* Olympia, WA: Office of State Superintendent of Public Instruction, Special Education.

Epstein, J. L. (1985). Home and school connections in schools of the future: Implications of research on parent involvement. *Peabody Journal of Education, 62*(2), Planning the School of the Future: Proceedings of a National Study Conference, 18–41.

Epstein, J. L. (2001). *School, family and community partnerships: Preparing educators and Improving schools.* Boulder, CO: Westview Press.

Epstein, J. L., Sanders, M. G., & Clark, L. A. (1999). *Preparing educators for school-family-community partnerships: Results of a national survey of colleges and universities.*

Baltimore, MD: Center for Research on the Education of Students Placed At Risk/Johns Hopkins University.

Gonzalez, M., & Chrispeels, J. H. (in press). No parent left behind: The role of parent education programs in assisting families to actively engage in their children's education. *The Elementary School Journal.*

Gonzalez, M., & Rivero, E. (2006). *The power of education programs for Latino parents: Increasing college education and leadership of Latinos in California.* Invited presentation at the II National Latino Education Summit in Puerto Rico, March 26–28, 2006. Retrieved November 20, 2006 from http://leadership.education.ucsb.edu/publications.html

Gonzalez, N., & Moll, L. C. (2002). Cruzando el Puente: Building bridges to funds of knowledge. *Educational Policy, 16*(4), 623–641.

Hackmann, D. G. (1997). *Student-led conferences at the middle level.* ERIC Clearinghouse on Elementary and Early Childhood Education, University of Illinois.

Henderson, A. T. (2007). *Beyond the bake sale: The essential guide to family-school partnerships.* New York: The New Press.

Henderson, A. T., & Mapp, K. (2002). *A new wave of evidence: The impact of school, family, and community connections on student achievement.* Austin, TX: Southwest Educational Development Laboratory.

Herrity, V., Ho, H-Z., Dixon, C. N., & Brown, J. H. (2006). *The Verizon OPTIONS Initiative: Supporting families' multiple literacies.* Paper presented at the American Educational Research Association Meeting, San Francisco.

Hiatt-Michael, D. B. (Ed.). (2005). *Promising practices for family involvement in schooling across the continents.* Greenwich, CT: Information Age Publishing.

Hong, S., & Ho, H-Z. (2005). Direct and indirect longitudinal effects of parental involvement on student achievement: Second-order latent growth modeling across ethnic groups. *Educational Psychology, 97*(1), 32–42.

Hoover-Dempsey, K. V., & Sandler, H. M. (2005). Final Performance Report for OERI Grant # R305T010673: *The Social Context of Parental Involvement: A Path to Enhanced Achievement.* Presented to Project Monitor, Institute of Education Sciences, U.S. Department of Education, March 22, 2005.

Hoover-Dempsey, K. V., Walker, J. M. T., Sandler, H. M., Whetsel, D., Green, C. L., Wilkins, A. S., & Closson, K. (2005). Why do parents become involved? Research findings and implications. *The Elementary School Journal, 108*(2), 105–130.

Hunt, C. (2002). *Guess who's coming to dinner: The impact of home visits on English language learners in a multicultural high school.* http://gse.gmu.edu/research/lmtip/arp/vol3.htm

Keith, T. Z., Keith, P. B., Quirk, K. J., Sperduto, J, Santillo, S., & Killings, S. (1998). Longitudinal effects of parent involvement on high school grades: Similarities and differences across gender and ethnic groups. *Journal of School Psychology, 36*(3), 335–63.

Mattingly, D. J., Prislin, R., McKenzie, T. L., Rodriguez, J. L., & Kayzar, B. (2002). Evaluating evaluations: The case of parent involvement programs. *Review of Educational Research, 72*(4), 549–576.

Moles, O. C. (1996). *Reaching all families: Creating family-friendly schools* (No. OAS-96-6005). Washington, DC: Office of Educational Research and Improvement.

Moll, L., Amanti, C., Neff, D., & Gonzalez, N. (1992). Funds of knowledge for teaching: Using a qualitative approach to connect homes and classrooms. *Theory into Practice, 31*(2), *Qualitative Issues in Educational Research*, 132–141.

Neuman, S., Caparelli, J., & Kee, C. (1988). Literacy learning, a family matter. *The Reading Teacher, 52.*

Nistler, R. J., & Maiers, A. (2000). Stopping the silence: Hearing parents' voices in an urban first-grade family literacy program. *The Reading Teacher, 53*(8), 670–680.

Paratore, J. R., Melzi, G. & Kroll-Sinclair, B. (1999). *What should we expect of family literacy? Experiences of Latino children whose parents participate in an intergenerational literacy project.* Newark, DE: International Reading Association.

Suarez-Orozco, C., & Suarez-Orozco, M. M. (2002). *Children of immigration.* Cambridge, MA: Harvard University Press.

Syverson, M. A. (2006). *Student-led conferences: Fourth-grade students and their parents' perceptions.* ProQuest/UMI, ISBN: 049693158X.

Weiss, H. B., Kreider, H., Lopez, M. E., & Chatman, C. M. (2005). *Preparing educators to involve families.* Thousand Oaks, CA: Sage.

Yeager, B., & Elder, PJ. (2005). Traveling the digital highway: Making complex connections visible. Retrieved October 15, 2006 from http://www.digitaldivide.net/articles/view.php?ArticleID=19

CHAPTER 6

PROVIDING CULTURALLY SENSITIVE PARENT EDUCATION PROGRAMS

Margarita Gonzalez, Hsiu-Zu Ho, and Kathy R. Fox

El beneficio era solidarizarnos e identificarnos más con nuestros hijos, maestros, y crecer. Aprender a comunicarnos mejor con nuestros hijos en ramo cultural y educacional para mejorar sus autoconfianza y valorizar sus raíces y a sus semejantes por un futuro mejor. En desarrollar arte, lectura, escritura, nos involucramos más en la educación de nuestros hijos.

The benefits [of this program] were to support and identify ourselves more with our children, their teachers, and to grow. Learn to better communicate with our children in the cultural and educational realm in order to increase their self-confidence and value their own cultural roots and those of their peers for a better future. In developing art, reading and writing, we involve ourselves more in the education of our children. (translated from Spanish, Parent, McKinley Family Stories Project, South Coast Writing Project, University of California, Santa Barbara)

Parent education is an umbrella term that encompasses a wide variety of programs geared toward educating parents on particular issues relevant to their children's development and schooling. These programs vary in both

Promising Practices for Teachers to Engage Families of English Language Learners, pages 87–117
Copyright © 2007 by Information Age Publishing
All rights of reproduction in any form reserved.

content and format, ranging from childrearing to academic programs and from group meetings to formal training. Parent education programs are considered "culturally sensitive" when the programs' goals, content and implementation, as well as the facilitators' attitudes and beliefs, reflect an understanding and appreciation of the families' unique values, beliefs and customs and their different ways of being and acting (Cheng Gorman & Balter, 1997). For example, in a culturally-sensitive parenting class, the facilitator acknowledges nontraditional childrearing practices and unique family constellations, and does not judge or compare the group's childrearing practices to mainstream standards.

One of the primary criticisms about the majority of parent education programs for English language learners (ELL) families is that the programs tend to be based on "deficit approaches," as noted in Chapter 2, rather than recognizing, valuing and building on the families' strengths. In employing deficit-based perspectives, a number of "intervention" programs unidirectionally focus on "teaching" parents the knowledge and skills needed to create positive home learning environments for supporting their children's education and development.

Parent education programs, however, can be more effective if they are provided in the form of professional development for families and teachers working together such that the teaching and learning are bidirectional. A culturally-sensitive parent education program respects and values parents' culture, traditions and education and incorporates the values and traditions of the participants. This type of program reflects a true "strengths-based collaborative model" between schools and families of English learners, in which the individual and collective social, intellectual and emotional capital is generated, the individual and collective sense of efficacy is enhanced, and a relational trust between schools and families is built (Chrispeels & Gonzalez, 2007). Researchers suggest that, while home learning activities are needed to enhance a child's learning, building social networks and relationships between teachers and diverse families as well as incorporating families' funds of knowledge into the classroom curriculum are also critical components of effective parent education programs (Boethel, 2003; Henderson & Mapp, 2002). Programs that focus on deficit approaches often fail to recognize the cultural and educational assets that diverse cultural groups possess. These deficit models tend to ignore the resources that immigrant families bring to our schools.

Lopez, Scribner, and Mahitivanichcha (2001) argue that we have to move from a "deficit mentality" and instead subscribe to a "strengths model" that effectively fulfills the educational needs of parents in ways that acknowledge and honor culturally relevant values, norms and understandings of their involvement. Their study on high-performing migrant-impacted schools presents effective practices that addressed the needs of migrant-farmer families from Mexico and facilitated the social capital that allowed them to negotiate the unfamiliar terrain of schools and the services available in the community. Based on an assessment of the families' needs, a school in Texas promoted informal talks or *pláticas* with their migrant-families that facilitated their awareness of the school system and home learning activities (Lopez et al., 2001).

The *Hmong Literacy Project* in Fresno, California is another example of a strength-based program. This school-site-centered program was initiated by Hmong parents who desired to acquire both first and second language literacy instruction (Kahn, Kuehn, & Herrell, 1996). Because Hmong has been a written language for only a few decades, the majority of the children in that particular community came from preliterate homes. The parents' goals were to be able to write down the oral traditions and histories of their Hmong culture before they were lost as well as "help their children academically and to narrow the disturbing rifts between the adults and child generations" (Kahn et al., 1996).

This chapter provides a variety of parent education programs for teachers and school personnel to consider. Teachers play an important role in fostering the home-classroom partnership by how they connect with diverse families and how they address the families' needs in sensitive ways. Delgado-Gaitan (2006) argues that a cultural broker (e.g., a teacher or parent liaison) is needed to help parents learn strategies for supporting their children's education and calls for "culturally sensitive programs" that address the parents' needs. Teachers are not expected to undertake a comprehensive parent education program in the school; they have neither the time nor the resources. Teachers need the support of school administrators, staff and community partners (e.g., parent liaisons, universities, community organizations) to promote parent education programs in their schools.

Culturally-sensitive parent education programs typically include activities and workshops in which families have the opportunity to share experiences as well as learn new skills to partner with their child's teacher. Teachers should create and maintain a family-friendly atmosphere in ELL parent education programs. Parents should be a part of the planning process so that program instructors or facilitators are sensitive to the needs and challenges that families may encounter in their new learning. Studies have found that parent education programs are more effective when the instructors share the same background as the participants (e.g., ethnicity, language) and have had similar experiences as parents (Chrispeels & Rivero, 2001; Lopez et al., 2001; Rivero, 2006).

PLANNING AND ORGANIZATION

Successful parent workshops require careful planning and implementation. Teachers need the support of school resources and staff in order to make parent education programs available to families of ELL. State and federal funding may also be a resource for such programs (e.g., Title I, Title III). For example, in California, the state legislature provided *Community Based English Tutoring* (CBET) program funding to local educational agencies and other institutions that enabled the implementation of family literacy and other English language development programs (California Department of Education, 2006). It is important to create and maintain a family friendly atmosphere when designing and implementing programs for families of English learners. Successful programs seek to learn about the needs and expectations of their students' families and actively involve parents and grassroots community organizations in the design and start-up phases of their programs.

PARENT NEEDS ASSESSMENTS

Successful, well-attended parent workshops often respond to the specific needs of parents. All too often when new programs are begun, the overall design for the school is predetermined rather than developed with family and community input. In order to avoid this, t is important to involve parents in the design phase of new parent programs or workshops. As discussed in Chapter 2, teachers need to have in-depth knowledge of their school community and use it in developing programs that address the particular needs of their ELL students and their families.

Determining the interests of parents requires a broad-based needs assessment, making sure to include opinions of parents who currently are not as visible at school events. A good way to informally assess the parents' needs and interests is through the Parent Conferences, which is one of the most attended parent events, particularly in elementary schools. Having some predetermined questions dealing with parent education options (e.g., *What types of events/classes would you like to attend? What aspects of our classroom/school would you like to learn more about?*) will help teachers to get a broad range of feedback to help with planning parent education events and will let parents know that their input is valued at the planning stages. Other informal needs assessments can be carried out via existing parent events, such as Back to School Night and children's performance events (e.g., Holiday Concerts). Parents can also be polled at school meetings, parent–teacher association and advisory council meetings.

There are several methods to formally assess the parents' needs: survey questionnaires can be sent directly to all parents at the beginning of the school year asking them to suggest topics of interest. For example, the *Verizon OPTIONS Initiative* (Herrity, Ho, Dixon, & Brown, 2006a) and the *Verizon Project SUCCESS* (Herrity, Ho, Dixon, & Brown, 2006b) in Goleta,

California were based on a needs assessment administered to all parents. The survey results indicated that English language development and helping their children with schoolwork were identified needs by the parents.

Parent liaisons and parent aides are also a good source of information and can be most effective in contacting parents. In a K–6 school in Minneapolis, teachers strived to involve parents of English learners in the very beginning design process of their workshops with the assistance of parent liaisons and aides (Gonzalez, 2004). Together, they conducted research on parent and family needs and expectations via telephone and written surveys. Through this process, they found that 95% of the parents surveyed responded that their workshops should focus on three areas: (1) academic activities at home (e.g., homework, math, reading); (2) discipline and behavior; and (3) effective communication between home and school. These three areas became the main guiding principles for parent programs at the school (Gonzalez, 2004).

Another way to gather data is to assess the opinion of school parents or community groups through public meetings and focus/study groups. Teachers may also provide a list of topics that they believe parents may be interested in or need to be informed about in order to navigate the school system and assess the need for their inclusion in parent education workshops. Such topics may include information regarding standardized testing, interpretation of test results, new grading system, and scholarship or college applications, etc. These lists can be distributed and discussed in one of the parent meetings in order to get the parents' feedback on the appeal and usefulness of the different topics.

PARENT EDUCATION LEADERS

Once parent needs are identified, resources (either internally or from outside agencies) necessary to meet these needs are examined. Resources may come from universities, businesses, social service agencies, regional education centers, or other institutions. Studies have found that parents are some of the best resources, as they are empathetic to the needs of the parent community and are able to relate to the demographic group at the school (Gonzalez, Chrispeels, & Rivero, 2006). Often when one or two parents assume leadership roles and assist with parent education activities, other parents become more willing to volunteer. Depending on the topic, workshop leaders may include: *specialists* (physicians, lawyers, speech therapists and social workers), *parents* (members of the parent group or the community who have the experience/skills to train other parents), *practitioners* (staff from community agencies and health clinics, members of church groups and volunteer groups, and paraprofessionals), and *educators* (university professors, teachers, school or district staff and community educators). Some schools can partner to jointly offer workshops that prepare parents as trainers. For example, the *PASSport to Success: A PASS training program* is a "Parent Trainer of Trainers" regional workshop that is offered in California. The 2-day training provides prospective parent trainers with the guidance and materials they will need to conduct parent training sessions based on the book *PASS: Parents Assuring Student Success* by John Ban (1993). It provides a step-by-step curriculum that includes specific instructional strategies, learning activities and dynamic PowerPoint slides for presenting material to parents. The curriculum covers the eight modules of the PASS book: parent attitude, home environment, study skills, homework and learning expediters, note-taking skills, preparing for tests, memory and thinking skills, and reading skills (Fresno Unified School District, *PASSport to Success*, 2006).

Some institutions offer programs for parent liaisons and parent involvement program leaders that prepare them to build strong parent programs and school-family-community partnerships. For example, the California Parent Center, in partnership with the San Diego State University College of Continuing Education, offers a *Parent Involvement Liaison Certificate Program* that provides a solid foundation for those new to coordinating parent involvement programs and strengthens the skills of experienced parent involvement staff. Through practical hands-on training and tools, participants learn (1) the latest research linking high quality parent involvement programs to improved student achievement, (2) research-based models for school-family partnerships, (3) parent recruitment strategies, (4) resources for making schools family-friendly, (5) specific roles for parent liaisons, (6) how to build on the strengths of culturally and linguistically diverse families, and (7) how to plan and implement high quality parent involvement programs at elementary and secondary schools. These activities directly support the schools' goals to improve achievement and meet *No Child Left Behind* (NCLB) requirements (California Parent Center, 2006).

RECRUITMENT OF PARTICIPANTS

An effective way to inform parents and enroll participants is to invite them to an orientation session. Teachers can hold meetings in their own classrooms, explain the content, activities, objectives, and rationale for the topics and strategies selected. Written notices or flyers may be sent to the homes to remind parents of workshops with a note regarding transportation and child care services. Children can help prepare flyers and invitations, and in this way be familiar with the information regarding the workshop as well. Word of mouth and a personal invitation from a child makes the invitation more meaningful and parent-friendly. A classroom newsletter may include articles on upcoming programs and can be followed by flyers that remind parents of the date, time, place, and topic of the workshop. It is important to circulate recruitment announcements in all languages spoken by parents at the school and posted in strategic locations such as neighborhood centers, churches, supermarkets, and laundromats. As suggested in Chapter 4, "telephone trees" may be useful in contacting and recruiting parents.

MATERIALS

Various types of materials should be prepared for families to address their diverse languages, literacy levels and learning styles. For example, the PASSport to Success program provides participant parents with a CD, a guidebook, a binder with written materials, graphs and visuals, and hands-on materials. The Prince George County Public Schools in Maryland has adapted a 17-page *Bookmarks for Parents and Teachers Ages Birth to 19 Years*, based on the *Parents Growing Together* and *Parenting Your Teenager* parenting skills programs from San Diego City Schools, California. These bookmarks are designed to assist all adults working with children in understanding the developmental stages of children and how to adjust programs to better meet their children's and teenagers' needs. These materials are available in English as well as Cambodian, Hmong, Lao, Spanish, Vietnamese, Somali and Tagalog and can be requested by phone or downloaded from http://www.fresno.k12.ca.us/divdept/cfen/ Flyer/BOOKMARKS%202004–2005.pdf (Prince George County Public Schools, *Comer SD Regional Center*, 2005). Schools can also prepare videos for parents that provide an orientation to the schools and community. In Alaska, the Fairbanks North Star Borough schools used their Title III funds to produce an Orientation Video for parents, titled *A Day at School*, that provides an orientation to the elementary schools. The video has been produced in three languages, Korean, Tagalog and Spanish, and an accompanying Orientation Guide has been translated in 13 languages. All elementary schools use the videos and guides to help ELL families become familiar with the school system (FNSBSD, 2006).

PROGRAM SCHEDULE

When planning the parent workshops, it is important to consider that in many low-income homes both parents work full time. Events may be held in the evenings or mornings to accommodate different work schedules. Gonzalez, Chrispeels and Arellano (2004) found success with a parent education program that was relatively brief—two hours per week for nine weeks. The *Verizon Project SUCCESS* offers a class three mornings per week for three hours at school while the school-age children are in class. The intergenerational family literacy program of Project SUCCESS is conducted throughout the academic school year and a summer session is offered. Attendance is consistently high with approximately twenty-four parent participants in the class (Herrity et al., 2006b).

PROGRAM LOCATION

A stimulating and comfortable schoolroom or library is an ideal place to hold the parent workshops. If possible, the room should be able to accommodate participants' movement between small and large groups with seating that can be arranged in a circle. While there are great advantages to holding the workshops in a school classroom, facilitators should be mindful that parents are treated as adults. For example, having adult appropriate seating and materials sends the message that parents are welcomed and valued. Ideally, the program should be offered at the local or neighborhood school to promote school connectedness and bonding. However, in certain areas where transportation to the school is not available for parents, an alternative location can be utilized, such as a local preschool or community center (Ho et al., 2004).

CHILDCARE

Childcare has been shown to be a cultural barrier for attendance at parent education events. Having a soft corner in the room for younger children to play safely is an easy alternative. A table with paper and crayons for the preschool age group is also easy to manage. For after school or evening events, school-age children may be supervised in an adjacent room with an instructional aide. Opening the computer lab for the school-age children during these events is an added incentive for families to attend. While younger preschool-aged children can be cared for in an adjacent space, parents should also be invited to keep their children with them. The Gevirtz Research Center *Family Literacy Program/ Isla Vista Youth Projects' School Readiness Program* offers a class jointly for adults and their preschool-age children. The focus is on English as a Second Language development for adults, while preschool children learn English and school readiness skills. Adults also learn strategies for helping their children at home with literacy development and schoolwork. The family literacy teacher and the preschool teacher plan together to develop joint parent-child activities for both the classroom and home (Herrity et al., 2006a).

TRANSPORTATION

Often, ELL families do not have their own transportation and this can prevent them from attending a particular program of interest. In a study conducted in 22 schools in Los Angeles, Gonzalez (2004) found that lack of transportation was one of the main barriers that prevented low-income immigrant parents from attending parent programs and school meetings. Teachers, support staff, or parent liaisons may help to organize transportation for their students' parents such as forming carpools; requesting a school bus or shuttle to the workshop; or, if feasible, reimbursing parents for bus fare. Many schools use their Title I funds to provide transportation to ELL and low income families to attend parent education programs and school meetings.

Multilingual Workshops

When there is a predominant ethnic group, it is more effective to have workshop leaders that speak the same language and/or be of the same ethnic background of the parents (Gonzalez & Chrispeels, 2005a). However, many schools have more than two languages represented by their ELL families. Schools may hire bilingual parents as their translators or train parents to be workshop facilitators. Some schools hold multilingual workshops in which the group reflects the cultural makeup of the school population. It takes a little more time to conduct multilingual workshops, but the added benefit is the opportunity to appreciate different cultures and languages.

TYPES OF PARENT PROGRAMS AND CONTENTS

There are many types of programs that may be offered to successfully meet the needs of families of ELL. Some of these programs are particularly designed for parents, while others promote parent-child or parent–teacher interactions. Following are descriptions of various types of parent education programs. These are not mutually exclusive programs; in fact many programs include some combination of the following types.

PROGRAMS ON NAVIGATING THE SCHOOL SYSTEM

Families of English learners are often unfamiliar with the U.S. school system, particularly at the high school level. Parents may feel intimidated about discussing curriculum concerns or other issues with teachers. This has led some schools to offer programs that enhance the parents' awareness of the school system. Information sessions may include the structure and function of the school, curriculum, academic standards, grading, standardized test assessments, health-related issues, after-school programs, and other programs that support English learners such as tutoring, mentoring, and homework clubs.

The *Parent Institute for Quality Education (PIQE)*, for example, offers several parent education programs in California and Texas. These programs equip low-income Latino and other ethnically-diverse parents to take an active role in their children's education (Chrispeels & Gonzalez, 2004). A seven-week program for Pre-K and kindergarten provides parents with information and activities for birth to five-year-old children that will help them develop a stimulating environment in their homes. The final goal is for the child to be well prepared upon entering preschool and kindergarten. Other PIQE programs include a nine-week session specifically designed for parents of elementary and secondary school students. This program covers topics that include the "ins" and "outs" of the U.S. school system and the basics of preparing for college (e.g., courses, applications, financial aid). After each session, parents are asked to apply the new information in a concrete way. For example, after learning about report cards, parents are asked to calculate their child's GPA based on the grades in their last report card (Gonzalez & Chrispeels, 2005a). Teachers interested in implementing this program in their schools can download the curriculum from PIQE website at www.piqe.org.

In the Howard County Public School System in Maryland, where a significant number of students are Korean, a series of seminars/workshops have been offered over the last decade to help parents to better understand the education system as well as help educators to better understand the culture of the participating families. The recent *7th annual Korean Education Seminar* featured a keynote address by a Korean immigrant who came to the United States as a high school student, struggled through many classes, and eventually gained admission to Harvard University (Zumbrun, 2006). The seminar included four workshops on parent strategies for helping students with writing assignments from elementary level to the SAT writing section. To better serve their large student population of approximately 50,000 students who are predominantly immigrants from 80 countries with 70 spoken languages, the Howard County school system has an Office of International Student and Family Services and employs twelve full-time bilingual community liaisons. Programs and services offered by this school system apparently have been successful in welcoming as well as attracting families from diverse backgrounds.

Cultural Awareness

Local communities and universities often sponsor multicultural activities and events that honor the diverse cultural heritages that immigrant families bring to the community. Many ethnic community-based organizations sponsor diverse educational, social and cultural programs that enrich the children's appreciation of their parents' cultural heritages (e.g., United Hmong Association of North Carolina, Casa de la Raza, Santa Ynez Band of Chumash Indians). Schools can partner with their local organizations to implement these types of programs. For example, the Fresno Unified School District in California offers a series of *Cultural Awareness Workshops* throughout the year to disseminate and celebrate the cultural heritages of each of their diverse family ethnic groups (e.g., African American, Mexican/Spanish, Hmong, Lao, Khmer) (Fresno Unified School District, 2006).

In connection with these events, teachers can also integrate specific cultural knowledge into the curriculum by inviting parents and community leaders to make presentations and undertake projects with students in their classrooms. Some of these activities may include cooking classes, celebrations of holidays, craft fairs, and festivals. For example, a high school in Sacramento, California, identified 25 different spoken languages in the school. Parents, students and school staff held monthly *Family Heritage Events* in which they learned about the diverse languages and heritages; the diverse cultural, family and social structures; the school systems in each country; the families' immigration histories and experiences in the United States; and their beliefs and expectations about the school. These events promoted the collaboration, tolerance and camaraderie among school staff, students and parents (B. V. Millhollen, personal communication, November 5, 2006).

Family Literacy

Family literacy programs stem from the philosophy that the parent is the child's first teacher and play a critical role in helping the child achieve educational success. The premise is that by establishing a program where the family is a partner in the child's education and is involved in educational experiences, there is a greater likelihood that the child will increase his/her educational achievement in school. Family literacy programs typically address oral and written language development skills using storybook reading, grammar development, readers' theater, interactive games and activities as well as technology. Materials used in the family literacy programs are often the same as those used by children in their classrooms. In this way parents learn the mainstream practices and academic language or "jargon" in order to better work with their children in mainstream academic areas (Gutierrez, 1995).

Some family literacy programs also include English as a Second Language (ESL) instruction. These differ from traditional ESL classes again because of the family focus, with the long-range goal of improving the child's literacy level by raising that of the parents. These "intergenerational literacy" programs coordinate the language education of parents with the education of their children (Amstutz, 2000; Morrow & Young, 1997).

Literacy and other adult basic education programs are very successful and typically have higher attendance when they are offered in conjunction with activities for children such as homework assistance and recreational activities. The Gevirtz Research Center's *Family Literacy Project*, for example, implemented three primary instructional components in eight Southern California elementary schools: oral and written English language development; parent support strategies for student learning; and family-school connectedness. A four-year quasi-experimental study of this project (Ho et al., 2004) showed improvement for participating parents in assessments of oral and written English language development, particularly, in knowledge of the language of homework directions. Qualitative analysis of class transcripts provided supporting evidence of participants' improvement in the use of oral English. Results for parent support strategies for student learning indicated that parents felt more effective in communicating with their children about school-related topics, spent more time helping with homework, and gained strategies for helping with literacy development. Parents also felt their participation had increased their children's motivation to attend classes and complete homework. Results of the family-school connectedness component showed recurring patterns of positive comments regarding parents' increased knowledge about, connection to, and comfort with the school. Moreover, the study demonstrated statistically significant benefits for children of participating parents. For example, differences were found between participant and comparison children for reading and language achievement scores favoring participants in Years 3 and 4. Qualitative results of parent perceptions were consistent with these findings (Ho et al., 2004).

An example of a consortium of multiple school-university-community partnerships that offered a comprehensive family literacy program to enhance multiple literacies is the *Verizon OPTIONS Initiative*, which subsequently expanded to the *Verizon Project SUCCESS* program. The first Verizon Initiative (Herrity et al., 2006a) offered an array of options, or literacy services (including English language development, school readiness for preschool children, parent education and advocacy, university tutors and mentors in the school and in homes, and computer literacy development) to ELL families to meet their needs. The Verizon Project SUCCESS (Herrity et al., 2006b) expanded the school-university-community partnerships to include a consortium of ten partners to address the complex literacy needs of ELL families. It offered integrated and targeted services that were effective in increasing school connections and involvement for language minority families and enhancing their multiple literacies.

Family Computer Literacy

Many parents are interested in learning computer skills and such classes have become popular and are often well attended by ELL families (Herrity, 2006a). Working together in a relaxed atmosphere provides parents and children an opportunity to gain valuable technology skills. These collaborative events, often held at school sites, help English learner families to gain self-confidence, be more involved in their school, and seek opportunities to support their children's education. A Parent Outreach Study conducted by the *Post-Secondary Access for Latino Middle-grades Students (PALMS)* reported the case of a mother and daughter who went through a computer class together (PALMS, 2005). As the mother's language and technology skills grew, so did her comfort level in communicating with teachers and administrators. This resulted in the mother becoming familiar with school-based resources, and eventually having her daughter identified as gifted and talented. Through the *Gaining Early Awareness and Readiness for Undergraduate Programs (GEAR UP)*, a collaborative effort of the U.S. Department of Education, the University of Texas at San Antonio and community partners, many middle and high schools in Texas provide computer literacy classes to English learner and immigrant families that meet in the evening once a week (UTSA, 2006). Childcare is provided for preschoolers, but the school-aged children can join their parents as they learn. The *Parents, Children, and Computers Project (PCCP)* is a computer literacy class that helps ELL parents learn how to use computers, software, the Internet and related technologies to publish articles and stories related to their cultural backgrounds and life experiences, as well as interests of family members. For example, one family wrote about its personal experiences in the course of navigating the school system and advocating for their child in an effort to obtain appropriate services for their child with special needs (Herrity et al., 2006a).

Family Math/Science Nights

Parents of ELL may find subject-specific information sessions to be useful in preparing them to better assist their children with homework. Such sessions provide the families with learning opportunities in specific curriculum areas taught in the classroom. Sessions can be organized around math, science, computers, creative writing, and other topics. Parents and students can work together with hands-on activities as well as be provided with further suggested activities to conduct with their children at home. For example, in a middle school in the Bronx, sixth-grade African-American students and their families got together on a weekly basis to work on hands-on science projects. After dining together, the families dispersed to different classrooms and spent the evening working on science activities that built upon what the students were studying in their science class. The program offered a number of options for extending the learning experiences beyond the school and into cultural institutions in their local area. The semester-long experience culminated with a special evening that gave families the opportunity to reflect on their experience in the program and exhibit their finished projects. The families' positive experience created a "buzz" in the neighborhood and resulted in the school having a large waiting list for next year's class of incoming sixth graders (PALMS, 2005).

In the Southern California science-based *Youth Enrichment Adventure (YEA) Program*, Family Days are held at the local botanic garden or neighborhood parks where ELL parents and students can engage in joint experiments focusing on the local ecosystem and watershed, as well as participate in the environmental restorative projects. The final celebration of YEA provides a family barbeque and showcases students' scientific investigations through group and individual presentations to parents and community members (V. Herrity, personal communication, October 23, 2006).

In New Jersey, the Rutgers Center for Mathematics, Science, and Computer Education (CMSCE) has assisted many teachers in implementing *Family Math* programs in their schools. These after school family involvement programs provide elementary school children and their parents with opportunities to develop problem solving skills and understanding of mathematical concepts in an enjoyable and nonthreatening atmosphere. Children and adults come together once a week for six weeks to do mathematics, and then practice at home ideas they learn in class. Using inexpensive hands-on manipulatives such as beans, toothpicks and coins, children gain a concrete understanding of space and numbers, develop problem solving strategies, and become more confident and willing to "tackle" new problems. All Family Math activities reinforce the New Jersey Core Curriculum Content Math Standards and include all math areas: arithmetic, numbers and operations, geometry, measurement, probability and statistics, calculators and computers, patterns, relations and functions, and logical thinking (Center for Family Involvement in Schools, 2006).

Programs on Parenting

Many social and developmental factors impact children and adolescents. Schools can assist in parenting by providing workshops that help families understand the needs of their children as they grow and develop. For parents of young children, issues surrounding their child's adjustment to new school routines and the social demands of school are often of great concern. Teachers can help by suggesting children's literature and activities for easing these pressures. Teachers may be asked for advice on issues such as a new baby in the home, sibling rivalry and how to juggle school, community and family responsibilities. Making your classroom library available, referring parents to other parents who might offer ideas, or just lending a sympathetic ear, shows a parent that the teacher is aware of parenting demands. One kindergarten teacher had a parent-lending library with books dealing with tough issues, such as death of a grandparent, divorce and the responsibility of taking care of a pet. The bilingual books on this shelf were children's picture books that could be shared between the parent and child to prompt discussions on these issues.

Parents of older children may benefit from being a part of group discussions, where they have opportunities to ask others—both professionals and other parents—how they are dealing with their own child's developmental changes. Important issues for them may include topics such as social realities of peer pressure, alcohol and other drugs, sexuality, racism, and sexism. Some issues such as teenage suicide, drugs, gangs and sexuality may not be typically discussed at home by some immigrant groups (Gonzalez & Chrispeels, 2005b). While at the same time respectfully acknowledging their cultural and religious beliefs, teachers may need to encourage parents to discuss these issues with their children. Schools may offer parent education workshops on topics such as understanding the impact of separation and divorce on children; developing a safe and secure environment for latchkey children; and handling the multiple roles of single parents. For example, the *Adolescent Wellness Family* course offered at Fresno Unified School District, California, is designed to help family members gain an understanding of the adolescent child. Throughout this course, family members learn helpful and practical skills that they can use to help them become more effective at parenting. Classes are once a week for 10 weeks in 3-hour sessions (Fresno Unified School District, 2006).

Father–Child, Mother–Child Groups

Fathers were often the "forgotten" and "missing" ones in family-oriented programs because mothers have traditionally been more involved in the schools and community organizations (Moles, 1996). However, in the last decades, there has been a growing recognition of the importance of the paternal role in child development, and more schools are trying to find meaningful ways of involving fathers. To promote father involvement and dispel any miss conceptions of parent involvement as a female-specific activity, some teachers organize father-oriented education events. Father-child study groups can promote the fathers' connection and support to their children's post-secondary education. In these events, fathers learn the various ways they can contribute to their children's learning and development and how teachers can assist them. Some of these topics may include tutoring students in academic subjects, exploring college and career opportunities, helping students learn nonviolent ways to resolve conflicts, understanding psychosocial development of adolescents and other issues regarding sex, drugs and health. Fagan and Iglesias (1999) found that a *Head Start Father Involvement Program* significantly increased the fathers' involvement at school and improved their children's school readiness. The program modified traditional Head Start parent involvement activities to make them more "father-friendly" (e.g., volunteering, weekly Fathers' Day programs, father sensitivity training with staff, monthly support groups for fathers, and father-child recreational activities).

Programs for mothers and daughters can also be successful. In Texas, many middle and high schools have implemented *Mother–Daughter Programs (MDP)*. The focus of these programs is to improve the mother/daughter relationship, personal growth, cultural awareness, community service, academic enhancement, and leadership skills. For example, the Junior League of Austin *Hispanic Mother–Daughter Program* offers four day-long events throughout the academic year for mother–daughter teams. The first event is a ropes course that allows girls and their mothers to work on team building and leadership, followed by community service day, and a college and career fair. The last event includes topics related to peer-pressure, self-esteem and substance abuse prevention, based on the *Soy Unica! Soy Latina!* (I am Unique! I am Latina!) education initiative of the U.S. Department of Health and Human Services. Each event is conducted in English and Spanish, followed by a time for the mothers and daughters to raise questions or voice opinions on the topic of the day. These events gave the participating mothers and daughters an opportunity to talk about some of the tougher issues, including sex education and birth control, which they normally wouldn't talk about. Other discussion topics included the desirability of attending colleges close to home versus those in other cities or states. These shared learning experiences had an impact on mothers' and daughters' perceptions of one another and of the people that could assist them in their pursuit of postsecondary education (The Junior League of Austin, 2006). Through this program, parents made valuable connections to personnel in the institutions that eventually helped them to put their daughters on the path to college (see Chapter 6 for other examples of Father–Son and Mother–Daughter programs).

Grade-Level Family Events

Teachers from the same grade level can join efforts and invite their classroom parents to an educational event geared especially for a particular grade level. Some of these events (e.g., getting ready for kindergarten) can occur during the summer prior to the beginning of the kindergarten year. Teachers can use their grade level meetings to plan this event together (Chrispeels, Andrews, & Gonzalez, 2007). Some topics may include: an introduction to a series of home-learning activities for use with their children; an introduction to a new curriculum program for the grade level; computer instruction with software used in their children's classroom; discussions of teen issues; and college bound curriculum, college preparation and applications.

College Camps

Parents of ELL are very concerned about what's next for their children after high school, but often do not know the university system and the resources available for their children to attend colleges and universities. In recent studies conducted by the Pew Hispanic Center (2004) and the Tomas Rivera Policy Institute (Tornatzky, Cutler, & Lee, 2002), 96% of Latino parents indicated that they expected their children to attend college but did not know the requirements or have knowledge about financial assistance for college.

Programs that address the transition to work after high school, college selection and financial assistance, and related topics need to be provided to parents with children at all grade levels so their planning for the future can begin in a timely manner. Some pre-college programs are very successful for helping parents to navigate the high school and university system. For example, the *ENLACE (Engaging Latino Communities for Education)* program is conducted in seven states (Arizona, California, Florida, Illinois, New Mexico, New York, Texas) with the goal of increasing the number of Latino graduates from high school and college. It is a coalition of grassroots community organizations that includes universities, community colleges, PK–12 schools, community-based organizations, students and parents. The *ENLACE y Avance* (Get Ahead) program sponsored by the University of California Santa Barbara, works with parents and students to put children on the path to the university. Through workshops, parents learn about the specific requirements that their children must complete in high school to be eligible for the university (ENLACE, 2005). In Los Angeles, California, after attending a parent workshop on "the road to the university," all ELL parents expressed greater expectations for their children's education, particularly that their child would go on to higher education. For example, a Latino parent commented how these workshops changed his interactions with his children:

> "My children and I talk more now. I ask them more about the future, what they want to study . . . the profession they would like to take in the university, so they can have a good job later. After the classes, I became more interested. I am more aware that I have to talk to them more about the future, since I have a child that is going to start high school" translated from Spanish. (Gonzalez & Rivero, 2006)

Many schools hold college camps or college nights for junior high and middle school students and their parents to assist them in preparing for college. Speakers from different universities and community colleges are invited to present information regarding their programs as well as financial aid packages that are available for minority students and first generations going to college. Professionals from different fields representing diverse ethnic groups are also invited to talk about their professions and their academic and career paths. Workshop participants also visit local universities. These events motivate families and children to aspire and make plans toward a college education.

Parent Tutors and Mentors

Many parents have volunteered to be tutors or mentors to students at risk of failure, knowing that these students especially need positive adult role models. The tutoring and mentoring programs can take place in business, community, and school settings. Schools also are developing community service programs and other creative opportunities for students to go into the community and learn by working with adults. The *Gevirtz Academic Mentor Program* provided school-based academic mentoring to elementary and junior high school students in Southern California which resulted in increased academic achievement, motivations for school, and aspirations for higher education and future careers (Rumberger, Brenner, & Herrity, 2002). Some states provide special funds for schools to prepare ELL parents as tutors. For example, in California the Community-Based English Tutoring (CBET) program is funded by the state to support free or subsidized English language instruction to parents or other community members who pledge to provide English language tutoring to California school children with limited English proficiency. The funds may be used for direct program services, transportation, materials or related services (California Department of Education, 2006).

Parents can also be mentors to other parents to assist them in negotiating the school system and communicating with school staff. Parent mentors can also help schools with parent involvement and communication. The Fairbanks North Star Borough School District in Alaska has implemented the *Parent Mentors* and the *Alaska Native Education (ANEA) Liaisons* to help schools overcome barriers to parent involvement. The Parent Mentors help families by calling about absences, greeting students and parents, and making home visits. The ANEA Liaisons provide students and parents with academic and personal support, and assist schools in communicating with parents (FNSBSD, 2006).

Parent Leadership

Parents of English learners that come from different school systems are not likely to assume leadership roles at school or classroom. Schools can help parents to develop leadership skills. Some parent leadership programs include topics such as the parents' rights and responsibilities at school, the structure and function of the school and district, how to access the media, how to make presentations; as well as field trips to school board meetings and city council meetings. Through its National Parent Partnership Program, the Mexican-American Legal Defense and Educational Fund (MALDEF) provide a 16-week leadership program for parents and a 4-day "*trainer of trainers*" for program instructors. Both programs are provided free of cost to schools in the states of California, Georgia and Texas (Gonzalez & Chrispeels, 2007). Teachers interested in implementing these programs in their schools can contact MALDEF or visit their website at www.maldef.org/psp (see chapter 6 for more information on parent leadership programs).

Family Resource Center

Auerbach (2002) recommends that schools provide "safe spaces where parents can learn, share and reflect on stories with fellow parents, sensitive educators, and others who look like them" (p. 1388). In some schools, there are parent centers or family resource centers which serve as meeting spaces for parent groups and workshops and individual parent–teacher or parent-principal discussions. These centers support parents in their development as both learners and teachers. They provide a space where parents can get together with other parents and school staff to learn how to assist their children's learning at home. A parent center can be used for different purposes; for example, to recruit and enroll parents in education programs, to train tutors and classroom volunteers, to connect parents with other educational or community agencies; to hold informal meetings or gatherings with parents, as lounges and waiting rooms for parents while they are in school, etc. As a family resource center, diverse materials may be available for parents and children including: a parent communication board with information of current school programs and events, higher education opportunities, cultural and community services and agencies which aid families with educational, health, and social service needs; reading materials to help parents guide their children's learning; games, books, and videos that parents can use with children at home; an exchange box where parents and teachers can drop off books, toys, and household items to share with others. If resources are available, comfortable furniture, a computer, coffee machine and other amenities can help to create a welcoming environment and working space where the families feel a sense of belonging to the school. Parent resource centers can be easily implemented in a spare classroom or a corner of a school library.

Another way to provide families with resources, particularly to low-income parents and those that often do not come to our schools, is to implement *Family Mobile Resource Centers*. These mobile centers can be implemented in a school bus or van and equipped with books and materials from the school library and/or donations from local bookstores or community partners. Mobile resource centers have been successfully implemented in several states in recent years, particularly to address the needs of migrant, low income, and homeless families. In New York, the Syracuse City School District has implemented a *PUMP (Power Unit for Motivating Parents) bus*, staffed by a parent advocate and three parent liaisons, to reach out to parents in the evenings and weekends. The bus "seeks out parents where it can find them" in the community, whether at local festivals, shopping areas or outside the city hall. This bus provides a variety of free, new and diverse books for parents and their children (infants to 12th grade), as well as home learning activities for various ages and grade levels, and local agency information. The goal of this project is to support learning at home and assist parents to help their children meet the New York State academic standards. Through this project, the schools have addressed two vital components of their Family and Community Involvement Policy, home-school communication and learning at home (Carter, 2003). In California, the Fresno Unified School District implemented a *Family Center on Wheels* that offers childhood health services, family support and family education for preschool children and their families. This mobile center visits neighborhood parks, businesses and churches three days a week (Fresno Unified School District, 2006).

Parent Support Groups

Parents with limited English skills do not often participate in school programs due to language barriers. In addition, many ELL families are low-income and parents are typically working at least one job and some are single. Creative approaches that address their situations and provide more specialized support are needed to help them become partners in the classroom. Strategies that are sensitive to these circumstances may include small study groups for these parents (e.g., a single-parent study group). Schools can involve parents in school programs by recognizing the families' need to have peer support during critical periods of their lives (e.g., their children's adolescent years, spouse's death, single parenting). Many parents appreciate the opportunity to share approaches and perspectives on single parenting issues. Schools can hold special parenting workshops and various seminars for divorced, widows/widowers, single parents and grandparents to address their particular needs. In *Verizon Project SUCCESS* (Herrity et al., 2006b), parents organized a Preschool Advisory Committee, to assist other parents with early childhood educational needs and advocate for additional preschool services in the district. Some national and local organizations work with schools and teachers to sponsor initiatives aimed to support single parents, particularly fathers. The National Fatherhood Initiative provides a variety of programs for single fathers and couples such as the *24/7 Dad Program* and the *Dads Club*. The 24/7 program consists of a comprehensive set of twelve 2-hour session fatherhood programs that can be conducted in school settings or in one-on-one home settings (National Fatherhood Initiative, 2006).

Parent Clubs

Workshops can also be provided through local parent clubs. For example, the *Parents Involved in Excellence (PIE)* is a club in North Carolina for parents with children (PIE, 2005). Teachers and guidance counselors from the local schools work closely with each PIE club. Because parents in this organization have many opportunities to interact with teachers, they often serve as parents' first point of contact when their child is having a problem at school. The PIE-affiliated teachers then become a bridge to other staff, guiding parents to the places where they can get the help they need. Through the efforts of PIE, parents become more confident in approaching their school. Many PIE clubs have established a strong presence at their local school, and PIE parents have assumed leadership responsibilities in their Parent–Teacher Associations. The support of parent volunteers is essential in operating the major programs such as *Saturday Academy* and *Summer Scholars* and in carrying out field trips. Regular meetings, newsletters, and telephone trees are used to keep parents abreast of program news and needs (PIE, 2005).

Community Study Groups

Some bilingual parent coordinators or volunteers meet with parents in their homes and at parent centers, churches, and other gathering places to inform them about school-related issues. Teachers or parent liaisons can draw on the community and facilitate the involvement of immigrant and working parents in their children's education by seeking cooperation and collaboration with resources in the community. Human service, cultural, social, and other organizations may aid in the development of programs and services that meet the needs of children and parents. One way is to enlist the aid of high school students and senior citizens with whom before- and after-school recreational and child care programs can be developed. Another way is to form partnerships with organizations that can provide programs for children, and work with employers to encourage them to institute flexible hours for working parents who want to attend school activities.

Community Resource Groups

Teachers may use the resources available in their communities and partner with community groups to support families of English learners. Teachers may contact community leaders and leaders from diverse ethnic groups to form multiethnic community resource groups. These groups can mobilize community resources to assist families in diverse aspects (e.g., health, economic, legal), as well as organize diverse educational activities in the school and community. For example, community resource groups can organize forums to discuss issues related to stereotypes and prejudice toward the school's ethnic populations so as to challenge any misconceptions about them. These events promote the social networks that ethnic-minority parents often need to help their children succeed at school. The University of California Santa Barbara Center for Teaching for Social Justice (now the Center for Education Research on Literacy Inquiry in Networking Communities, LINC) worked with the Building

Bridges Community Coalition in Santa Barbara to train families and students as docent partners (as well as teachers and students) for an exhibit called a *Slave Ship Speaks* about the artifacts found from the wreck of the Henrietta Marie. This kind of intergenerational learning and work, facilitated by family, university and community partnerships, enables partners to both share and gain new expertise and knowledge (Ho et al., in press). In Oregon, the Child Center, a family-based agency, provides various services for children with emotional and mental disorders, pregnant teens, and mobile resource libraries for children and families. The *Mobile Resource Library* travels to each region every three weeks throughout the year. The mobile resource library van is stocked with literature, videos, and books to loan and disseminate to interested community members (The Child Center, 2006).

Homework and Home Learning

The literature in the field of homework consistently states that the best practices for homework involve some degree of parent involvement. However, this involvement may mean different things to different parents. In the literature, homework is sometimes characterized as a potentially traumatic event (e.g., *Homework Without Tears*, Canter, Hausner, & MacMahon, 1988) or as a hassle for the family (Beaulieu & Granzin, 2004). Frequently, the parental involvement is more supervisorial; for example, establishing clear expectations for the completion of homework and related consequences. The mainstream view is that the goal of homework is to help children become independent learners; that is, in charge of their own learning (Beaulieu & Granzin, 2004).

In a study of homework practices in ELL families, homework was found to be a collective family activity and identified as a significant source of English print used by all families in the study (Fox, 2003). The data from home visits made visible common themes across seven participating families. Homework was seen as a collective family activity in all cases. Younger children (pre-K) participated by drawing, writing, and interacting during the school-age child's homework time. Older siblings shared homework and other school materials with younger children. Parents cited this practice as an intentional homework strategy. Older children were observed routinely helping younger ones with their homework. The place or setting of the homework was also noted in the home visits. In each of the seven cases homework was conducted at a family/group area, as opposed to an individual desk. In none of the seven cases was a quiet setting with an individual lamp or desk used, as was suggested in school and family literacy class communication as well as the literature on best practices for homework (Beaulieu & Granzin, 2004; Rosado, 1994; Teft, 2000; Unger, 1991). Instead homework was central to the family activity. The language of the homework activity was negotiated between English and Spanish, using both for clarification and home language maintenance. The study revealed that homework was a family focus with multiple goals and benefits rather than an individual event. Unpacking of the school bag each day provided access to English print and mainstream practices. The parents' roles in maintaining and valuing the home language were evident in the actual work of the homework activity, as the written work was orally explicated and made tangible in the home language (Fox 2003).

What teachers of ELL can do to help children be more successful in their homework is to recognize the importance of parent involvement. With the increased significance placed on homework, teachers are given a "nightly" opportunity to reach out to minority language parents. The homework communicates not only the progress of the child but the curriculum of the classroom. Teachers can use homework as a way to learn more about the children's families and home life. One homework program invites families to rotate open-ended projects through the families, with each parent and child adding a page. When it is the child's turn to take home the Family Story Book, not only does he get the chance to write and draw with his family an entry about his own family, but he also gets to see and read what other children and families in the class have contributed. Samples of these projects are:

- *Family Fiestas*: Draw a picture and write about a family celebration.
- *Family Pets*: Draw a picture of a favorite family pet that someone in the family has had; write about its name, where it came from and why it was loved.
- *School Days*: Ask your family about schools today and in the past. On one page draw your school today, on the back of the page draw your parent's school, and on the next page, draw your parents/grandparent's school. On the back of that page tell how these schools are alike and different.

Families should be given more than one day to complete this type of projects. When the child returns back to school with the project, it is passed to another child in the class. This strategy takes only a little time to prepare on the teacher's part, but yields big benefits in the information that teachers and families learn about each other.

Home Learning Support

Events can be held to promote learning at home and include topics such as helping with reading, limiting television viewing, providing space and time for study, learning materials and educational games, tutoring skills, computers and others. Some teachers hold ongoing training for groups of parents who want or need intensive help with home learning. Others visit parents in their homes to provide individualized assistance with home-learning activities for students at risk.

Teachers generally need extra time to develop ideas for activities and materials that parents can do at home to address the needs of ELL students. Teachers can designate a bilingual parent volunteer to serve as *Home-Learning Coordinator* to help organize and reproduce home-learning materials, ensuring that these activities are developed for home use and from an additive, rather than a deficit, language perspective.

Teachers can also organize *Parent Homework Networks* to promote afternoon and evening homework sessions. These sessions are particularly useful for single or working parents. Several parents can host a group of children on a rotating basis and provide them with a supervised and quiet place to study and do homework. These networks require much coordination such as might be provided by a parent liaison, volunteer, or release time teacher. Help facilitate the expansion of parent networks. Schools can help parents connect with each other and expand their social and educational network. Ultimately this connection can build parents' knowledge about and interest in involvement practices to support children's academic success (Weiss, Kreider, Lopez, & Chapman, 2005).

PROGRAM EVALUATION

Schools with strong parent education programs evaluate their programs to assess whether they were effective, how they might be modified, what contents and activities may be added, and what recruitment and enrollment efforts may be more effective to reach more parents. Three useful ways to obtain parent feedback regarding program effectiveness are via evaluation forms, focus group discussions, and parent journals. After each session, parents may be asked to fill out a brief *evaluation form* that includes three basic questions: what worked well or was most useful; what did not work or was least useful; and what they would like to get more of or other topics/programs they would like to have provided. A second way to obtain parent feedback is to conduct *focus group discussions* either in the middle and/or at the end of the workshops. Open discussions in the middle of the program can provide rich data that will help to modify the program in a timely manner and prevent high attrition rates. During these group discussions parents may be asked open-ended questions that facilitate discussion including what parents are learning and applying at home and school, barriers they face in their involvement at school and/or classroom, and ways the workshops may be enhanced/improved (Gonzalez & Chrispeels, 2007). These focus groups usually provide in-depth understanding about many aspects of the program. For example, data gathered from focus groups in the *Gevirtz Research Center Family Literacy Project (FLP)* revealed that as a result of participating in the program, participants felt better informed about school activities and more comfortable communicating with their children's teachers and other school personnel; they were better able to interpret written communication from their children's schools; they felt more effective in communicating with their children about school-related topics; they spent more time helping their children with homework; and their participation in the FLP had increased their children's motivation to attend classes and complete homework. Participants were also asked what changes they would like to see made to improve the program. Some parent participants responded that they would like more opportunities to practice their oral English. This information was shared with the FLP teachers and resulted in several instructors including more opportunities for oral interactions in their classes. When asked what might prevent other parents from attending classes, most parents indicated that time conflicts and family illnesses were the factors most likely to stop parents from attending. Parents at one school noted that lack of transportation was a problem for many families at the school. Based on this information, the school subsequently provided a bus service for participants the following year. Other parent comments included: "Because of the class, I know what activities are scheduled at school so I can participate in them." Another parent stated, "I feel more confident when I have to do something at my child's school." "Now we are well informed," said another parent; "The teachers now count on us" (Ho et al., 2004).

A third way to obtain parent feedback regarding programs is via parent journals. Parent journals are powerful tools that can be used for several purposes: (a) to assign homework activities that parents may engage in at home and/or school after each session (e.g., read with child, visit a university, contact the teacher or counselor); (b) to evaluate each session of the program; and (c) to record parent insights from a particular event or activity (e.g., "how I advocated for my child and enrolled him/her in a GATE program"). In an evaluation of a parent leadership program for ELL families, Gonzalez and Chrispeels (2007) designed a *Parent Leadership Journal,* which was translated to the parents' home language and printed in the form of a booklet. Parents enjoyed writing in their journals about their learning experiences in the program, and how they applied this new learning in their everyday lives, in their interactions with their children, teachers and administrators, and their participation in their children's classroom and school. Program leaders (instructors) used these journals as an instructional tool. During the first 10 minutes of each session, parents shared their journal with a partner, and some volunteered to share it with the whole class.

CONCLUSION

In this chapter we have offered a variety of strategies and programs that teachers and administrators can implement in their classrooms and schools. While some of these activities are widely used in many schools, we have provided various ideas and approaches for building on the strengths and the diverse cultures that ELL families bring to our classrooms. While we have included a number of programs that have been proven to be most effective for ELL families, space limitations impede us to include many other exemplary activities. It is our hope that beginning and experienced teachers will implement a number of the activities included in this chapter and share with us their successes. We also hope to hear your suggestions and ideas on other types of parent education programs and strategies that are most successful with ELL families. We believe that schools with strong parent education programs are more likely to establish better relationships and partnerships with ELL families, and consequently, improve student learning.

QUESTIONS

1. What parent education programs and workshops do your ELL families need in order to be successful partners in their children's education?
2. Are these parent education needs currently being met by your school and community? If not, what can you as a teacher do to help facilitate the development of such programs?
3. What are some of the ways your school can improve to better meet the needs and expectations of families of your English learner students?

REFERENCES

Amstutz, D. (2000). Family literacy: Implications for public school practice. *Education and Urban Society, 32*(2).

Auerbach, S. (2002). Why do they give the good classes to some and not to others?: Latino parent narratives of struggle in a college access program. *Teachers College Record, 104*(7), 1369–1392.

Ban, J. R. (1993). *Parents Assuring Student Success (PASS): Achievement made easy by learning together.* Bloomington, IN: National Educational Service.

Beaulieu, J. E., & Granzin, A. (2004). Taking the hassle out of homework: How to make homework a more positive experience for your child. *Our Children Magazine, 25*(2), 9–13.

Boethel, M. (2003). *Diversity: School, family, & community connections* [Annual synthesis]. Austin, TX: Southwest Educational Development Laboratory. Retrieved September 1, 2005 from http://www.sedl.org/pubs/catalog/items/fam35.html

California Department of Education. (2006). Community-Based English Tutoring (CBET). Retrieved November 26, 2006 from http://www.cde.ca.gov/sp/el/cb/

California Parent Center. (2006). *California network of partnershipsSchools, June Burnett institute for children, youth and families of San Diego State University Foundation.* Retrieved November 22, 2006 from http://parent.sdsu.edu/

Canter, L., Hausner, L. & MacMahon, B. (1988). *Homework without tears: A parent's guide for motivating children to do homework and to succeed in school.* New York: Harper Collins.

Carter, S. (2003). *Educating our children together: A sourcebook for effective family-school-community partnerships.* Eugene, OR: CADRE, Consortium for Appropriate Dispute Resolution in Special Education. Retrieved November 21, 2006 from http://www.directionservice.org/cadre/EducatingOurChildren_01.cfm

Center for Family Involvement in Schools. (2006). Rutgers Center for Mathematics, Science and Computer Education (CMSCE), Family Math. Retrieved November 22, 2006 from http://www.rci.rutgers.edu/~cfis/index.html

Cheng Gorman, J., & Balter, L. (1997). Culturally sensitive parent education: A critical review of quantitative research. *Review of Educational Research, 67*(3), 339–369.

Chrispeels, J. H., Andrews, C., & Gonzalez, M. (2007). System supports for teacher learning and school improvement. In T. Townsend (Ed.), *International handbook of school effectiveness and improvement* (pp. 787–806). London: Springer. Retrieved November 22, 2006 from http://leadership.education.ucsb. edu/publications.html

Chrispeels, J. H., & Gonzalez, M. (2004). Do educational programs increase parents' practices at home? Factors influencing Latino parent involvement. Research Digest. *Harvard Family Research Project,* Graduate School of Education, Harvard University. Retrieved October 10, 2006 from http://www.gse.harvard.edu/hfrp/projects/fine/resources/digest/latino.html

Chrispeels, J. H., & Gonzalez, M. (2007). No parent left behind: The role of parent education programs in assisting families to actively engage in their children's education. Manuscript Submitted to *The Elementary School Journal.* Retrieved November 22, 2006 from http://leadership.education.ucsb.edu/publications.html

Chrispeels, J. H., & Rivero, E. (2001). Engaging Latino families for student success: How parent education can reshape parents' sense of place in the education of their children. *Peabody Journal of Education, 76*(2), 119–169.

Delgado-Gaitan, C. (2006). *Bulding culturally responsive classrooms.* Thousand Oaks, CA: Corwin Press.

ENLACE (2005). *Engaging Latinos for college education.* ENLACE Newsletter, January 2005. Retrieved November 10, 2006 from http://www.vancomm.com/ enlace/ january2005/index.html

Fagan, J., & Iglesias, A. (1999). Father involvement program effects on fathers, father figures, and their Head Start children: A quasi-experimental study. *Early Childhood Research Quarterly, 14*(2), 243–269.

Fox, K. (2003). *Constructing mainstream academic discourse practices in home- and school-based settings.* Unpublished dissertation. University of California, Santa Barbara.

Fresno Unified School District. (2006). *Community and family engagement network.* Retrieved November 21, 2006 from http://www.fresno.k12.ca.us/divdept/ cfen/ index.html

FNSBSD. (2006). *Fairbanks north star borough school district, family and community.* Retrieved November 22, 2006 from http://www.northstar.k12.ak.us

Gonzalez, M. (2004). *Factors affecting Latino family involvement in K–12 schools.* Paper presented at the Language Minority Research Institute (LMRI) conference, Santa Barbara, California. Retrieved November 1, 2006 from http://leadership.education.ucsb.edu/publications.html

Gonzalez, M., & Chrispeels, J. H. (2005a). *Effects of parent education programs: Knowledge, beliefs and practices of Latino families in middle schools.* Paper presented at the American Educational Research Association (AERA) annual meeting in Montreal, Canada. Retrieved October 25, 2006 from http://leadership.education.ucsb.edu/publications.html

Gonzalez, M., & Chrispeels, J. H. (2005b). *Building school communities through education programs for immigrant families.* Presentation at the International Congress for School Effectiveness and School Improvement (ICSEI), Barcelona, Spain. Retrieved October 10, 2006 from http://leadership.education. ucsb.edu/publications.html

Gonzalez, M., & Chrispeels, J. H. (2007). *Evaluation of the National Parent Leadership Program of the Mexican-American Legal Defense and Educational Fund (MALDEF).* Invited presentation at ARCHES/ENLACE Family/Community Networking and Best Practices Workshop, Long Beach, California.

Gonzalez, M., Chrispeels, J. H., & Arellano, B. (2004). *Evaluation of the effectiveness of the Parent Institute for Quality Education in Los Angeles Unified School District,* September 2003 to May 2004. Evaluation Report. Retrieved November 15, 2006 from http://www.piqe.org/assets/specialprj/program%20evaluation. htm

Gonzalez, M., Chrispeels, J. H., & Rivero, E. (2006). *Designing parent programs, and research and evaluation for parent involvement programs.* Invited presentation at the California ENLACE Family/Community Networking and Best Practices Workshop, Santa Barbara, California. Retrieved October 1, 2006 from http:// leadership.education.ucsb.edu/publications.html

Gonzalez, M., & Rivero, E. (2006). *The power of education programs for Latino parents: Increasing college education and leadership of Latinos in the United States.* Invited presentation at the National Latino Education Summit, San Juan, Puerto Rico. Retrieved November 1, 2006 from http://leadership.education. ucsb.edu/ publications.html

Henderson, A. T., & Mapp, K. L. (2002). *A new wave of evidence: The impact of school, family and community connections on students' achievement.* Austin, TX: National Center for Family and Community Connections with Schools. Available at http://www.sedl.org/connections/resources/evidence.pdf

Herrity, V., Ho, H-Z., Dixon, C. N., & Brown, J. H. (2006a). *The Verizon OPTIONS initiative: Supporting families' multiple literacies.* Paper presented at the American Educational Research Association Meeting, San Francisco, CA.

Herrity, V., Ho, H-Z., Dixon, C. N. & Brown, J. H. (2006b). *The Verizon Project SUCCESS: Sustaining university and community collaboration to promote educational success in school.* Invited presentation at the National Family Literacy Conference, Louisville, KY.

Ho, H-Z., Dixon, C. N., Brown, J., Herrity, V., Tomlinson, H. A., Fox, K. R., Luo, Y-H., & Humerez, S. (2004). *A four-year study of family literacy: Promoting parent support strategies for student success.* Paper presented at American Educational Research Association, San Diego, CA.

Ho, H-Z., Yeager, E., Green, J. L., Dixon, C. N., Tomlinson, H. A., Desler, G., & Rogers-O'Reilly, J. (in press). Archeology of a Virtual Tour: Uncovering the layers of student engagement with complex issues of race in digital space. *Screening Noir.*

Junior League of Austin. (2006). Hispanic Mother–Daughter Program. Retrieved November 21, 2006 from http://www.jlaustin.org/

Kahn, H-W., Kueh, P. & Herrell, A. (1996). The Hmong Literacy Project: Parents working to preserve the past and ensure the future. *The Journal of Educational Issues of Language Minority Students, 16.* Retrieved October 11, 2006 from http://www.ncela.gwu.edu/pubs/jeilms/vol16/jeilms1602.htm

Lopez, G. R., Scribner, J. D. & Mahitivanichcha, K. (2001). Redefining parental involvement: Lessons from high-performing migrant-impacted schools. *American Educational Research Journal, 39*(2), 253–288.

Moles, O. C. (1996). *Reaching all families: Creating family-friendly schools.* Washington, DC: Office of Educational Research and Improvement. Retrieved September 15, 2006 from http://www.ed.gov/pubs/ReachFam/iraf.html

Morrow, L., & Young, J. (1997). A family literacy program connecting school and home effects on attitude, motivation, and literacy achievement. *Journal of Educational Psychology, 89*(4), 735–742.

National Fatherhood Initiative. (2006). *Dad program.* Retrieved October 10, 2006, from http://www.fatherhood.org

PALMS. (2005). *Parent outreach study.* Post-Secondary Access for Latino Middle-grades Students, PALMS Project. Retrieved October 6, 2006 from http://www.palmsproject.net/reach/

Pew Hispanic Center. (2004). *National survey of Latinos: Education.* Washington, DC: Pew Hispanic Center/Kaiser Family Foundation. Retrieved September 6, 2006 from http://pewhispanic.org/reports/surveys/

PIE. (2005). *Parents involved for excellence.* Retrieved September 25, 2006 from http://www.unc.edu/depts/cmse/pre_college/pie.html

PIQE. (2006). *Parent Institute for Quality Education, Parent Programs.* Retrieved October 10, 2006 from http://www.piqe.org

Prince George County Public Schools. (2005). *Department of family and community outreach and strategic partnerships*. Retrieved January 15, 2005 from http://www.pgcps.org/~dfamcoms/index.html

Rivero, E. (2006). *A study with an ethnographic perspective: A new perspective on Latino families and their children's schooling*. Unpublished Dissertation. University of California, Santa Barbara. Retrieved November 1, 2006 from http://leadership.education.ucsb.edu/publications.html

Rosado, L. (1994). Promoting partnerships with minority parents: A revolution in today's school restructuring efforts. *The Journal of Educational Issues of Language Minority Students, 14*.

Rumberger, R. W., Brenner, M. E., & Herrity, V. A. (2002). *Can mentoring improve academic achievement? An evaluation of a four-year early adolescent program*. Final report to the California Department of Education.

Teft, L. (2000). Excluded voices: Class, culture and family literacy in Scotland. *Journal of Adolescent and Adult Literacy, 44*(2).

The Child Center. (2006). *Mobile Resource Library*. Retrieved November 22, 2006 from http://www.thechildcenter.org/about.html

Tornatzky, L.G., Cutler, R., & Lee, J. (2002). *What Latino parents need to know and why they don't know it*. Claremont, CA: Tomas Rivera Policy Institute.

Unger, H. (1991). *What did you learn in school today? A parent's guide for evaluating your child's school*. New York: Facts on File.

UTSA. (2006). The University of Texas at San Antonio, Gear Up Office. Retrieved November 21, 2006 from http://www.utsa.edu/gearup/whatis.cfm

Weiss, H. B., Kreider, H., Lopez, M. E., & Chapman, C. M. (Eds.) (2005). *Preparing educators to involve families: From theory to practice*. Thousand Oaks, CA: Sage Publications Inc.

Zumbrun, J. (2006, October 19). A two-way street for immigrants, *Washington Post*. Retrieved November 20, 2006 from http://www.washingtonpost.com/wp-dyn/content/article/2006/10/18/AR2006101800747.html

CHAPTER 7

ENGAGING PARENTS AS LEADERS IN SCHOOLS WITH ENGLISH LANGUAGE LEARNERS

Judith Munter, Josefina Tinajero, and Antonio del Campo

Maria Rios, an immigrant mother from Guatemala, and her husband Francisco work at low-paying agriculture jobs. Their four children attend public school and have had considerable difficulty keeping pace with other children in their respective classrooms. In a family night event, Maria spoke with student teachers about her own motivation to provide the opportunities for her children that she herself never had... "I've been here in the U.S. for 6 years. Ever since my children started going to school, I've been interested in helping them to develop their intellectual potential. When they stay home, they just watch TV and play. My daughter used to just stay in bed and sleep. Going to school gives them more energy. I have told them that they have great opportunities and they need to pay attention and do their best. Especially us... as Mexican parents, we want to do everything to give our children the opportunities that we never had. I do everything I can to motivate them. One day I took my daughter with me on the bus to see the University. I told her, before you get married, you need to get your schooling and have a profession. This is your future!"

Promising Practices for Teachers to Engage Families of English Language Learners, pages 119–133
Copyright © 2007 by Information Age Publishing

119

This vignette illustrates the importance of listening to family members within the school community. Informal interviews, such as this one, play a critical role in informing teachers about the dreams of mothers like Mrs. Rios.

CHALLENGES AND OPPORTUNITIES

Need for Understanding of Cultural and Linguistic Diversity in Schools

Like many school systems worldwide, U.S. schools are being altered by steady high flows of newcomers as children of immigrants tripled their share of the K–12 student population between 1970 and 2000. The English language learners (ELL) student population rose between 1993 and 2003 by 84 percent while the overall student population rose 12 percent. These ELL are often concentrated in urban schools that are highly minority, low income, and disproportionately likely to fail federal standards (Fix & Capps, 2005).

One of the challenges faced by school districts everywhere is finding staff, faculty, and others in school planning and policy decision-making teams who can authentically represent the voices of the increasingly multicultural parents and students. Parents and community members are an untapped resource with significant potential to address the growing need for bilingual literacy educators and advocates for bilingual education in growing numbers of communities throughout the nation. Their common experiences are a significant resource, which can more than compensate for nonnative speaker status. Schools that provide the most effective programs of study for ELL integrate human and physical resources from the local community to contribute to the school's learning environment. The significant knowledge and understanding possessed by many parents and extended family members, including their familiarity with learners' cultural and linguistic backgrounds, life experiences, and community issues are an untapped resource for curriculum development.

A critical research finding is that the highest achieving schools for ELL have built strong linkages with parents and others in the community (Southwest Educational Development Laboratory, 2003). Effective schools in communities with diverse populations have embraced new models that empower parents to seek venues for active contribution to transform the educational community. In these schools, parents from different educational backgrounds feel welcomed in every classroom and know that they can make significant contributions to the educational process of their children, regardless of their educational level or ability to speak English. Thus, teachers should utilize programs that encourage new models of parent involvement, rather the traditional roles of passive parental involvement. These new models will provide family members with opportunities to develop their leadership skills. Parents need to understand how the school relates to the larger community and learn strategies for making interactions between school and community mutually supportive and beneficial.

What happens at home and in the time outside the classroom is either going to reinforce, complement, or undermine that which is going on inside the classroom. An important part of our role as teachers is help parents and other teachers in our schools to realize that it is in everyone's interest to engage parents as full partners. Parents of ELL can become leaders of school improvement and strategic planning. An important role of the teacher is to find and nurture connections with those parents who have this kind of imagination, this kind of curiosity, who care deeply, and are willing to recognize that everyone benefits when parents and teachers work together as a team.

Maria Rios, the immigrant mother who has become integrated into the life of her child's school, is taking on new leadership roles and illustrates the potential for teachers to connect with these parents' dreams and hopes, in spite of language or background differences. Parents can help teachers understand the dreams and vision of ELL children and their families. From this perspective, all in the school setting benefit, diverse language, culture, or ethnic differences are viewed as assets, and teachers become uniquely prepared to develop a strong and effective partnership with the community.

Support for Family Involvement in School Leadership

Public schools are public institutions, an expression of society's commitment to development of young people and the education of our children. Leadership logic and leadership action (Cisneros, 2006) are key principles at the heart of efforts to develop learning communities that engage public school personnel in partnership with parents as leaders in the K–12 classroom. The most effective schools serving large populations of ELL successfully have found ways to go beyond parental involvement in school activities, to parent engagement (i.e., the development of parents as leaders). In such schools, teachers learn to collaborate with parents in new ways. Parents find that they are not just extra helpers in school projects and activities. As teachers and parents work together, they set up strategic teams that are empowered to plan, implement, and evaluate activities that can have a transformative effect on the entire school community.

In their book on the teaching gap, Stigler and Hiebert (1999) contend that although some critics of U.S. public schools have pointed to the Japanese approach to classroom pedagogy a viable solution, when American teachers try to import methods that work well in Japan, they do not get the same results. Their research points out that U.S. educators need to recognize that the Japanese teaching method is encased in a culture and a set of traditions. Parents' and communities' values and expectations play a major in role in defining the work that is done in local schools; if those expectations are not changed, then adopting a different teaching technique is not going to do much. What does matter is enabling students and their parents to have ownership over their own education; what matters really is how teachers, parents, and the children themselves develop authentic relationships with school personnel, thus changing the culture of the school (Senge, 2000).

Parents as leaders tend to respect and value local cultures, listen deeply, engaging others in the variety of new roles that extend far beyond bake sales and fundraisers. They accept responsibility for advocating for the rights of all children. In towns and cities on the U.S./Mexico border as well as in Hispanic urban communities, parents have informed these authors how their commitment to education embraces the entire community. By learning to establish equitable teaching/learning environments, caring about all children and not just one's own sons and daughters, parents, and schools become part of community action and community change. These parent-leaders value collective action above personal recognition and develop collaborative relationships with other parents as they prepare to take on leadership roles.

From this perspective, parents develop leadership skills by working in groups, planning and carrying out activities, speaking in front of groups, and developing other personal skills and traits that support community development. The emphasis is on collective action, listening to peers, and revolving tasks and leadership roles.

Parents and Teachers as Agents of Community Change

In many communities where ELL reside, numerous issues are waiting to be addressed. These may cover a wide range of areas—from getting a stop sign on the corner near a school to building a playground area to any number of other things. Parents can work with school personnel to develop leadership teams that engage in mobilizing other families and community members around identifying needs, developing action plans, and implementing change.

Teachers can do much to encourage parents to participate in their children's education, keeping in mind that active participation of families in the life of the school matters more than parental income or educational background. Parents' efforts to help their children learn can impact their children's achievement than family income or education. This is true whether a family is rich or poor, whether parents finished high school or not, or whether children are in preschool or in the upper grades (Educate America Act, 2000).

"Out-of-School" Time: Leading Community Outreach

Much of what young people learn occurs in "out-of-school" hours (Bartko, 2005; Weiss, Coffman, Post, Bouffard, & Little, 2005) and parents' roles as educational leaders may be most evident in the community/home environment. In communities where families come from diverse backgrounds and speak languages other than English, parents as leaders can guide teachers, college students, and other school personnel as they develop plans for relevant learning in local contexts and implement field trips and community service learning projects/activities. Teachers who work in schools with ELL need to be responsible for initiating the contact and reaching out to the community, because parents and families of ELL students frequently are not familiar with U.S. systems, and may not know how to reach out and engage with the schools.

Our responsibility as professional educators is to create an environment where we reach out to parents and to community member and give them opportunities to forge meaningful connections with the school. Each time a teacher (or student teacher) communicates with parents, letting them know how much they are valued as partners with important knowledge and expertise, new opportunities for student achievement and school improvement result. Many parents of ELL do not realize that they are both welcomed and needed in the school system.

There are many ways schools can reach out, but it is critical to build that partnership with different people. Some schools hold social nights for parents and teachers to get to know each other. Other schools invite parents to come into the classroom for specified periods to engage in reading time with children in their own native language. The role of native language literacy in developing academic proficiency is critical for children who are nonnative speakers of English and *parents as experts* can help schools set the tone for welcoming all ELL children into the community of learners, engaging their families as full members and valued participants in school-community activities. This is an ongoing process because schools with large populations of ELL are always dealing with new populations and must be open to ongoing learning with the community. Table 7.1 provides an example of an effective classroom activity to engage parents and extended family members as effective leaders and conveyors of knowledge in the classroom.

TABLE 7.1
The Oral History Night

Residents of Canyon Valley are immigrants from Mexico and Honduras. The majority of these hard-working adults have had limited experience with formal education, and describe themselves as hesitant about their own qualifications to make a difference in their children's education. They are adamant believers, however, in the critical role that education can and will play in providing opportunities for their daughters and sons to improve their lives. Oral History Nights events have provided a platform for lively and enriching exchanges of family history, 'funds of knowledge', and cultural exchanges. Parents, grandparents, and all extended family members are invited to the school/community center, and as part of the event, these community members bring photographs that can help them to tell the unique story of their own family's journey, accomplishments, sacrifices, and unique experiences. With their own children and college students in the storytelling circle, these individuals open new doors to understanding for all involved. The conversation is guided with questions such as:
• Tell me about the place in which you were born.
• What was it like growing up in name of town/city?
• How did you (or relatives) come to the decision to leave your home to travel to this country?

PARENT LEADERSHIP ACTIVITIES

Impacts on Classroom Curriculum

Parents of ELL are important conveyors of knowledge, history, experience, and values; they are uniquely qualified to work with teachers in planning and implementing innovative approaches to teaching/learning in the school's curriculum. For example, community members may be unaware of the benefits of well-designed bilingual education programs. There are tremendous opportunities here for teachers and parents with bilingual skills and knowledge to work together to develop packages of information that will enable other parents and families to understand the rationale for teaching children to be well grounded in their native language and well informed about their native culture, family histories, etc. Parents of ELL are well suited to this work and many have become leaders in their own and others' communities in disseminating this information effectively.

A classroom activity that can engage parents and teachers in dialogue about the rich resources that immigrant families bring to the school community is the Oral History Night (see Table 7.1). This event is developed and led by the families.

Community Service Learning

Community outreach through service-learning activities can offer powerful possibilities for linking with educators' goals for enhancing research and improving practice. Community service-learning, at its best, engages the resources of schools and universities in helping communities to build bridges of mutual understanding among parents of diverse cultural, ethnic, and linguistic backgrounds. Inviting parents to the school/community center for these student-led events can work well as a venue for service-learning projects, such as Parent Power Nights.

Parent Power Nights are a series of sessions are held at regular intervals to engage pre-service teacher education students and in-service teachers with parents in open communication. They have included activities that provide the college students with unique opportunities to promote and support parents' leadership skills, enable parents to learn strategies that can help them assist student learning, and enhance diverse skills and knowledge that parents posses. Parents are encouraged to attend "Parent Power Nights" with their family members to learn how to enhance quality time together and share fun academic activities. These activities are designed, planned, and implemented by pre-service teacher education students.

In some communities, home visits provide opportunities for providing service, enhancing learning and generating new knowledge about diverse communities including the values, vision, and background knowledge that parents and families possess (see Chapter 1 of this monograph for further discussion of home visits).

The Family Story Power Writing Workshop

Teachers who recognize the effects of family life on school performance sometimes lack practical ways to include families naturally in children's academic progress. This workshop gives clear guidance for showing K–5th grade students' parents activities to do at home that will help children achieve success in writing. It also shows teachers how to offer projects that inspire families to actively encourage children's writing efforts.

The Family Story Power Writing Workshop brings students' parents, grandparents, and other relatives into the school's computer lab to produce a book of family stories. The workshop shows adults how to help their children increase verbal and writing skills through family storytelling, art, and children's writing at age-appropriate writing levels. Parents relate childhood memories and K–5th graders illustrate the stories. Family members collaborate to write the story on the computer (by themselves or by dictating to helpers). After the workshop, the written stories and illustrations are scanned and comb bound into books. An autograph party celebrates the publication, and each family receives a copy.

The workshop provides numerous outcomes. The following are major findings from this activity:

1. Parents and children have new incentives and inspiration for writing at home by seeing their collaborative family writing efforts published.
2. Parents have learned about their child's writing level.
3. Parents and children practice working together to retell a family story using art and writing at the child's age-appropriate writing level.
4. Parents and children have had an opportunity to share their family stories by having them collected and published in a book.

The Mother–Daughter Program

In its 20th year, the Mother–Daughter program is a collaborative partnership between parents and teachers from eight low-income school districts on the U.S./Mexico border—urban and rural, large and small. This program was developed with the express purpose of empowering Hispanic girls and women, providing them with the support and resources needed to enable them to achieve their educational and professional goals. The program works closely with the University of Texas at El Paso (UTEP). Over the past 20 years, the program has transformed the lives of hundreds of young Hispanic women and their mothers. With a primary focus on young girls from grade 6 through the freshman year in college, the Mother–Daughter Program instills in these participants high aspirations for educational achievement and career success. Mothers are coequal participants with their daughters, learning how to help the girls succeed and advance themselves academically and professionally. The program organizes activities for the girls and their mothers around four broad goals: (1) Encouraging girls to complete their high school education and to raise their expectations of attending college; (2) Orienting the girls to higher education and professional careers; (3) Improving the quality of preparation for higher education by providing academic and life-skills training; and, (4) Increasing Hispanic parental commitment to higher education by involving mothers as well as daughters in the educational decision-making process. The Mother–Daughter Program provides an inspiring example of how young women from low socioeconomic backgrounds, many of whom are recent immigrants and are learning English as a second language, can break educational and career barriers. Maria, El Paso, TX, reveals:

Life has been anything but easy for my mother, my brother, and me. Even though we have struggled, I always remember my mom being there for us. She always told us how important school was and she used herself as an example...The Mother–Daughter Program came into our lives. It helped Hispanic girls like me...anyway, my mom was going to be there with me, and that made me feel better...

Parent Bilingual Advisory Committees

As mentioned in Chapter 4, parent advisory committees are mandated in *No Child Left Behind* (U.S. Department of Education, 2002). In California, for example, all schools are required to have a Bilingual Advisory Council to ensure that academic needs of ELL are met. However, opening the school to get parents to participate on these committees requires strategy. One teacher organized "Breakfast with the Principal" and opened the school media center for one hour twice a month (M. Gonzalez, personal communication, October 18, 2006). When at first only the most involved parents attended, the principal moved the breakfast to a table in the foyer of the school. In this way, she was able to meet, greet, and involve more parents as they dropped off their children. After a few of these more assertive invitations the breakfast became more inclusive and eventually helped to form the Bilingual Advisory Committee.

In a Family Learning Literacy Program in Pasadena, CA, the Parent Bilingual Advisory Council plans, organizes, and implements several events a year (J. Espinoza, personal communication, October 16, 2006). Teachers have met with this group and support the parents' leadership. Members of this committee assume full responsibility for holidays and festivals. For example, members of the Council decided to have a winter holiday play. Teams of parents were organized to select a story or play, sew costumes, make stage props, provide music, and handle refreshments. Other events have been a Fathers' Day pancake breakfast, a spring school wide festival, or songs around the world. Teachers invite parents into classrooms: Egyptian parents taught counting in Arabic, Russian parents led folk dances, and Chinese and other families read stories in their native language. An assessment of alumni parents revealed that 87% had volunteered in other situations after leaving this program.

We have observed a variety of parent leadership programs. Some parent leadership programs include organizational issues such as how to organize transportation for school events or how to make appointments for meeting with teachers. Other programs focus on family services issues, such as how referral services work within the school and other support agencies, the parents' rights and responsibilities at school, or the structure and function of the school and district. Some provide instructional tools, such as how to access media, teach computer search skills, or how to make presentations. Lastly, family leadership programs provide field trips to school board meetings, city council meetings, or state conferences.

University–School District Collaboration Model

To improve opportunities for a comprehensive program of parent development, Canutillo Independent School District in collaboration with The University of Texas at El Paso, provides a good example of a school–university–community partnership that is working to increase the quality and scope of effective parent engagement in a linguistically diverse community. All parties involved recognize that this collaborative work is the cornerstone of a strength-based approach to student development to increase ELL students' personal and academic achievements. Educational partnerships provide the best means for the parents of children who are ELL to move from passive participation to leadership roles in their schools and communities. A major premise of this process of parent empowerment is acknowledgment, validation, and valuing of parents of ELL. Family members serve the following roles:

1. the first teachers of the children;
2. resources to the school;
3. decision makers within the school; and
4. trainers of other parents.

Canutillo Independent School District (ISD) teachers have worked in collaboration with the University of Texas at El Paso in planning and implementation of activities that promote parental involvement. In Canutillo ISD, parents are encouraged to actively participate in a variety of activities to help them become resources, decision-makers, trainers and leaders of others in their own community. Examples of Canutillo ISD and The University of Texas at El Paso active parental and pre-service teachers' involvement activities are displayed in Table 7.2.

SECURING TRAINING FOR PARENT LEADERSHIP

Teachers have options of prepared training programs for parents. The Mexican-American Legal Defense and Educational Fund provide a 16-week leadership program for parents and a "trainer of trainers" free of cost for schools. More information can be gathered from www.maldef.org/psp.

TABLE 7.2
Active Parental and Pre-Service Teachers' Involvement Activities

Time to be a Parent:	Family members are invited to attend panels to talk about personal issues and share their concerns about the education that their child is receiving. Through collaborative inquiry, community members have learned to develop effective parent engagement plans, take action, and reflect on their experiences. Techniques such as panels and small-group discussions are used to enable family members and future teachers to view school-community relationships through new lenses and vision parents as full partners in the decisions that affect children and schools. Families receive the benefit of small group contact and support. Pre-service teachers gain authentic learning experience with parents and students. The role of the future teachers is to be moderators and assure that the meeting is conducted in a professional manner.
Mi Decision Tambien Cuenta (My Decision Counts too):	This project honors the active participation of ELL parents and family members in the decision-making process of our programs. Family members are integral constituents of the School Advisory Committee Team, Ad Hoc Committee, and Task Force Committee. These committees convene on a regular basis throughout the school year. The committees provide valuable and significant guidance to program staff concerning important issues, such as such program design and implementation. Parents' comments and suggestions are taken into consideration and their contributions enrich the services that the district provides to the students.
Parent Institute:	This event is held annually to promote the active participation of parents and family members in an event similar to a conference. The planning and designing process of the institute is accomplished by a group of parents/leaders who dedicate their time and effort to planning, implementing, and evaluating all key aspects of the institute. The "Parent Institute" is an advocacy event for parents and family members intended to facilitate activities designed to assist parents become effective partners in their children's education.
Parents as Presenters:	Our parents of ELL are continually developing their capacity to become presenters at national, state, and local levels. Parents promote greater understanding of the academic, social, cognitive, and linguistic needs of their own and others' children who are ELL by sharing personal stories and topics relevant to the issue of diversity from a variety of perspectives, including cultural perspectives, and diverse family structures.

In California's Isla Vista community, a number of Latino parents receive leadership training through the Padres Adelante (Parents Moving Forward) program, a key component of the ENLACE y Avance initiative run by the University of California, Santa Barbara (ENLACE, 2005). The program uses a curriculum that covers topics such as parents' rights and responsibilities, the structure of the school system, how to conduct a meeting, and how to make an effective presentation. The program, first run at Isla Vista Elementary School, has now expanded to include a middle school and a high school. Initially conducted by an ENLACE staff member, the training is now run by parents who graduate from the program.

Padres Adelante graduates have found a number of ways to make their voices heard in the community. Several participants formed a task force and met regularly with the principal at Isla Vista Elementary to discuss the need for more nutritious food for their children. The task force successfully advocated to the district for the addition of a salad bar to the school's cafeteria. Parents also met with representatives from a local foundation to express their support for a proposed new neighborhood playground. The grant was approved, due in large part to the parents' leadership role in the process.

CONCLUDING REMARKS

Parent/leaders participating in various parent leadership program share that the described activities and processes have created more communication among parents. In addition, these activities provide parents the skills to organize events, plan effectively, become involved in the education of their children, the opportunity to unite two different cultures, and better opportunities to work together and learn from one another.

A solid partnership among homes, schools, and communities is foundational to the success of various legislative or local education initiatives. Parents and community groups need to be encouraged to participate actively as members of schools' learning communities. This approach defines school improvement as a collaborative enterprise, characterized by shared vision, collective inquiry, teamwork, an orientation toward action, commitment to continuous improvement, and a focus on results (Eaker, DuFour, & Burnette, 2002). The most effective schools are intrinsically connected to parents and community members who are involved in meaningful ways with the processes of school improvement and change. Linking school programs, for example, with the lived experience of students' families and their own unique community history can contribute to transforming and revitalizing the curriculum (McCaleb, 1997; Perez, & Torres-Guzman, 2002).

While the projects and programs described in this chapter focus primarily on discussion of Hispanic families and children, the key principles of communication, trust, use of native language(s), respect for family cultures and history, and celebration of diversity are applicable to teachers' work in a wide number of culturally/linguistically diverse schools and communities. In work with Native Americans, for example, respect for the community elders requires teachers' attention and time. Rather, than developing preconceived plans and timelines. Beginning educators establish trust and enhance communication in schools with ELL and their families by learning to listen carefully and respectfully.

Far too often, family members in low socioeconomic communities with limited English skills feel that the language barrier is a factor that impedes their active participation in school activities (Nieto, 2002). Instead of perceiving this challenge as a barrier, however, effective schools with high percentages of ELL students (such as Canutillo ISD) make accommodations to serve all in their community as equal individuals in our society. Key areas have been identified which require special attention based on the perceived needs and priorities of the parents of ELL. These include: (a) supporting parent organizations; (b) raising awareness among parents in empower them to educate and influence public attitudes toward bilingual education; and (c) the development of materials in two (or more languages) to assist parents to learn how to become actively involved in the education process.

Classroom teachers play important roles in promoting change and improving schools. They can also help to strengthen the parents' knowledge about the roles of native language literacy and bilingual education in U.S. schools. As our school populations become increasingly diverse, new and experienced teachers can play an important role in school improvement plans by engaging parents of ELL as leaders in partnership with schools, universities and community organizations to support underserved student populations.

High-achieving schools with culturally, linguistically diverse student populations recognize the importance of developing effective and creative approaches to encouraging participation and celebrating family members' roles in the educational process (Delgado-Gaitan, 2004; Jesse, Davis, & Pokorny, 2004; Ramirez, 2003). Many of the best school improvement initiatives reflect advances in the educational community's understanding that family units are diverse, all families are important and the roles that families play in children's intellectual and social development are invaluable. In schools with culturally, linguistically diverse populations, parents' leadership in decision-making processes is critical to the development of effective and high achieving schools.

Educators concerned with issues of equity and the academic achievement of diverse students (Banks & Banks, 2004; Jesse et al., 2004; Nieto, 2002) have advanced a number of recommendations for school personnel to implement in their schools, particularly when working with recent immigrants and their families. These include:

- Teachers should communicate a clear vision and mission; the belief that immigrant students can succeed and attend college should be at the core of all programs, activities and policies;
- Teachers should develop programs that provide opportunities for after-school tutoring and mentoring programs, inviting and encouraging family members to participate whenever possible;
- Parents should be encouraged to become actively engaged in the life of the school and in their children's education. A wide variety of options should be made available to accommodate diverse families' life styles, work hours, and weekly schedules (Gonzalez, Huerta-Macias, & Tinajero, 1998; Mapp, 2002; Turner-Vorbeck, 2005);
- Families and community members should have opportunities to extend their vision of educational opportunities through activities that help them become familiar with higher education opportunities.

QUESTIONS

1. Which of the above activities could be implemented in your school? Who will you need to work with to plan, design, and implement the activity? How will you evaluate the effectiveness of the activity?
2. One of the programs that develop parents as leaders in school settings in El Paso, Texas is through outreach to the community, in programs like the Mother–Daughter Project. What are some of the outreach activities in your school-community?

REFERENCES

Banks, J., & Banks, C. (2004). *Multicultural education: Issues and perspectives.* New York: Wiley & Sons Publishers.

Bartko, W. T. (2005). The ABCs of engagement in out-of-school-time programs. *New Directions for Youth Development, 105,* 109–120.

Boethel, M. (2003). *Diversity: School, family & community connections.* Austin, TX: Southwest Educational Development Laboratory.

Cisneros, H. (2006, March). *Charting a course for Hispanic higher education.* Plenary Session conducted at the 1st Annual Meeting of the American Association of Hispanics in Higher Education, San Antonio, TX.

Delgado-Gaitan, C. (2004). Involving Latino families in schools: Raising student achievement through home-school partnerships. Thousand Oaks, CA: Corwin Press.

Eaker, R., DuFour, R., & Burnette, R. (2002). *Getting started: Reculturing schools to become professional learning communities.* Bloomington, IN: National Education Service. (ERIC Document Reproduction Service No. ED469431)

Educate America Act. Retrieved September 1, 2006, from http://www.ed.gov/legislation/ goals2000/theact/index.html

ENLACE (2005). *Engaging Latinos for college education.* ENLACE Newsletter, January 2005. Retrieved November 10, 2006 from http://www.vancomm.com/enlace / january2005/index.html

Fix, M., & Capps, R. (2005). *Immigrant children, urban schools, and the 'No Child Left Behind Act'.* Retrieved September 2, 2006, from the Migration Policy Institute Website: http://www.migrationinformation.org

Gonzalez, M., Huerta-Macias, A., & Tinajero, J. (Eds.) (1998). *Educating Latino students: A guide to successful practice.* Lancaster, PA: Technomic Publishing Company.

Jesse, D., Davis, A., & Pokorny, N. (2004). High-achieving middle schools for Latino students in poverty. *Journal of Education for Students Placed at Risk, 9*(1), 23–45.

Mapp, K. L. (2002). *Having their say: Parents describe how and why they are involved in their children's education.* Paper presented at the Annual Meeting of the American Educational Research Association, New Orleans, LA.

McCaleb, S. P. (1997). *Building communities of learners: A collaboration among teachers, students, families, and community.* Mahwah, NJ: Lawrence Erlbaum Associates, Publishers.

Nieto, S. (2002). *Language, culture and teaching: Critical perspectives for a new century.* Mahwah, NJ: Lawrence Erlbaum Associates.

Perez, B., & Torres-Guzman, M. (2002). *Learning in two worlds: An integrated Spanish/ English biliteracy approach, 3rd ed.* Boston: Allyn & Bacon.

Ramirez, A. Y. (2003). Dismay and disappointment: Parental involvement of Latino immigrant parents. *Urban Review, 35,* 93–110.

Senge, P. (2000). *Schools that learn: A fifth discipline fieldbook for educators, parents, and everyone who cares about education.* New York: Doubleday.

Stigler, J., & Hiebert, J. (1999). *The teaching gap: Best ideas from the world's teachers for improving education in the classroom.* New York: The Free Press.

Turner-Vorbeck, T. (2005, Winter). Expanding multicultural education to include family diversity. *Multicultural Education, 13*(2), 6–10.

University of California Santa Barbara. (2006). Office of Academic Preparation and Equal Opportunity (APEO). Retrieved November 2, 2006 from http:// www.apeo.ucsb. edu/ap/index.html

U.S. Department of Education. (2002). *No Child Left Behind act.* Retrieved September 18, 2006, from http://www.ed.gov/legislation/esea02

Weiss, H. B., Coffman, J., Post, M., Bouffard, S., & Little, P. M. D. (2005). Beyond the classroom: Complementary learning to improve achievement outcomes. *Evaluation Exchange, 11*(1), 2–6, 17. Retrieved from www.gse.harvard.edu/hfrp /eval/issue29/theory.html

ABOUT THE CONTRIBUTORS

Antonio del Campo UTEP Graduate Student, and a Canutillo Independent School District Lead Teacher, College of Education, University of Texas at El Paso, El Paso, TX. adelcampo@canutillo-isd.org

Chris Ferguson Program Associate, Southwest Educational Development Laboratory, Austin, TX. cferguson@sedl.org

Kathy Fox Assistant Professor, Language and Literacy, Watson School of Education, University of North Carolina, Wilmington, NC. foxk@uncw.edu

Margarita Gonzalez Director of Research and Evaluation, Gevirtz Graduate School of Education, University of California, Santa Barbara, CA. gonzalez@education.ucsb.edu

Diana B. Hiatt-Michael Professor of Education, Graduate School of Education and Psychology, Pepperdine University, West Los Angeles, CA. diana.michael@pepperdine.edu

Hsiu-Zu Ho Professor of Education and Psychology, Gevirtz Graduate School of Education, University of California, Santa Barbara, CA. ho@education.ucsb.edu

Judith Munter Associate Dean and Associate Professor, College of Education, University of Texas at El Paso, El Paso, TX. jmunter@utep.edu

Linda Purrington Lecturer and Director for the Educational Leadership Academy and Educational Leadership Administration & Policy Program, Graduate School of Education and Psychology, Pepperdine University, West Los Angeles, CA. lkpurrington@aol.com

Reyna- Garcia Ramos Associate Professor of Education, Graduate School of Education and Psychology, Pepperdine University, West Los Angeles, CA. reyna.g.ramos@pepperdine.edu

Josefina Tinajero Dean and Professor, College of Education, University of Texas at El Paso, El Paso, TX. jtinajero@utep.edu

Promising Practices for Teachers to Engage Families of English Language Learners, page 135
Copyright © 2007 by Information Age Publishing
All rights of reproduction in any form reserved.

Printed in the United States
107300LV00002B/336/A